# Olive Oil
## source of life

Editions Grecocard
**ATHENS 1998**
**FIRST EDITION**

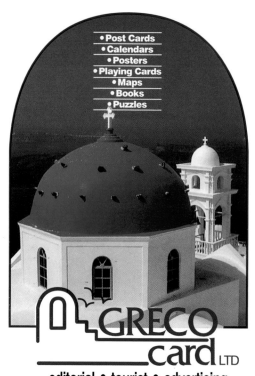

• Post Cards
• Calendars
• Posters
• Playing Cards
• Maps
• Books
• Puzzles

GRECO card LTD
editorial • tourist • advertising
3 Aglavrou str. 117 41 Athens, tel: (01) 9248292/293, Fax.(01) 9241910

Title:  Olive oil  source of life Greek Cookery
Editor: George Monemvasitis
General Editing and Supervision: Si Enorasis Advertising
Recipes and Texts: Aspasia Angelikopoulou - SEVITEL
Photography: Studio Gallegos - SEVITEL
Color Seperation: APOPSI
D.T.P. Si Enorasis Advertising
Montage:  F.Vrettas -X.Georgiadis LTD
Printing: Tipos Ellas S.A.
Printing: B.Eutaxiadis - I.Iosifidis
Main trading: **Greco Card LTD**
Canada: by Martin Publishing L.t.d
3 Parker Avenue, Toronto, Ontario, Canada, M8Z 4L6
Tel: (416) 259-8355, Fax: (416) 259-6930

ISBN 960-7436-44-X

*Dear Friends, Olive oil, old as our history and related to legends and traditions, has always been a irreplacable food for our people.*

*Consequently, even today the Greek is the largest consumer in the world of olive oil, since oil covers approximately 70% of fatty substances that are consumed.*

*However, this product that is so well-known and wide-spread, still remains an unknown factor for many people.*

*Recently, the promotion of comparable products by the mass media in our country has raised many questions. At the same time contradictory discussions by both experts and non-experts as to the biological value of olive oil, the calories and vitamins that it contains, the saturated and unsaturated lipids, the relationship of fatty acids with cardiovascular disorders, have added to the confusion and have caused misunderstandings.*

*This book was written because there is the need to clear up these misinformative conclusions created by insufficient information concerning olive oil and to give consumers effective and responsible data.*

*We believe that SEVITEL, with its many years of experience, its scientific knowledge of the subject and its many-faceted research on the product, is in the position to give complete and systematic information concerning olive oil; an essential product produced by our country, which brings in billions in revenue for our national economy and for which over 470,000 Greek families are involved in the cultivation of olives.*

*This book is just the beginning, in order that we may learn more about this blessed fruit that has flourished and has developed from the serene Greek coastlines to the highest regions of the land since antiquity.*

# Olive

# Oil

## Olive oil through the centuries

Historical Evolution

The origin of the olive and its fruit has been lost in the passing of time but it is certain that it evolved from the shores of the Mediterranean. Archaeologists have hypothesized that the cultivation of the olive began over six thousand years ago.

The Palestinians were known for their olives and olive oil which they exported to Egypt. The Egyptians began to cultivate olives around 1750 BC but production was not very large, nor of good quality.

However, the systematic cultivation of olives really began on the shores of the Aegean, the Greek peninsula and the coastline of Asia Minor.

Along the coastline of the Greek seas, the olive was extensively cultivated ever since the years of mythology. From the findings of Knossos (earthenware jugs and oil storage areas) it seems that around 2500 BC the Cretans used olives and oil in the same manner that we do today. They traded extensively with their neighbouring countries, thus developing their economy. At the palace of Nestoras in Pilo writings were found showing that oil was used as a form of payment for goods and services. A complete passage filled was also found with pieces of earthenware jugs for storing oil. Besides, the importance of oil is also mentioned in the "Athenian State" by Aristotle. His work refers to the fact that athletes taking part in the Panathenea were awarded splendid urns filled with oil from "Mories" olives. With Greece as its "birthplace", the olive spread to other countries in the Mediterranean, to Sicily, to the Iberian Peninsula and to the northern shores of Africa.

The British historian Alfred Zimmepn stated that the olive may be considered to be a native tree of Greece, and from here it spread throughout the Mediterranean, beginning from Italy in the 20th Century BC. Greek colonists also brought the olive with them to southern France, while the Romans passed it to Spain and Portugal. Finally, around the 16th C. the Spanish carried the olive with them to S. America, Mexico and the United States. In Australia the olive was cultivated by the British in the 19th C.

## Statistical data

Today the olive is cultivated on all five continents. Ten years ago the number of olive trees throughout the world was about 660 million. Today this number has reached 700 million olive trees, while the production of olive oil is 1,408,600 metric tons.
Of this amount, 81% is produced in Europe and the remaining 19% in other countries

throughout the world. Specifically, the Mediterranean countries cover 98.5% of the world production of olive oil (Table 1).
Italy currently leads world production with 32%, Spain is second with 31%, Greece third with 14%, Tunisia fourth with 6% and Turkey fifth with 4%. In the production of edible olives, Greece is first with 60,000 tons, followed by Spain, the United States, etc.

## Olive oil as a product for the Greeks

Ten years ago Greece had approximately 100,000,000 olive trees. Of these 75,000,000 were in the form of normal olive plantations while the remaining 25,000,000 were scattered among other cultivations. Today the figures should be about the same, because even though new olive trees are planted every year, trees with low productivity or trees presenting difficulties in the

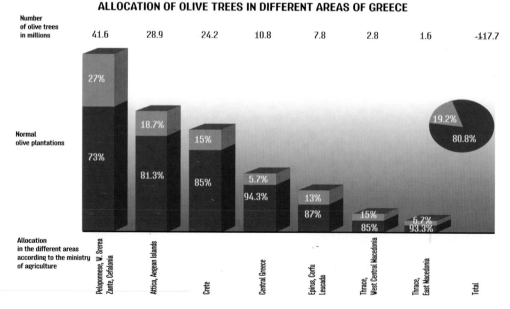

**UNIVERSAL PRODUCTION OF OIL** (half universal production of aperiod '79-'80=1.408.600ton. =100%

Pie chart labels: SPANE (30.7%), ITALY (31.9%), GREECE (14.4%), O.C.EUROPE (4.13%), TURKEY (4%), TUNISIA (6%), MAROCCO (2.5%), O.C. AFRICA (0.7%), USA & OTHER COUNTRIES

**ALLOCATION OF OLIVE TREES IN DIFFERENT AREAS OF GREECE**

| Number of olive trees in millions | 41.6 | 28.9 | 24.2 | 10.8 | 7.8 | 2.8 | 1.6 | -117.7 |
|---|---|---|---|---|---|---|---|---|

Bar chart values — Normal olive plantations:
- Peloponnese, W. Srerea Zante, Cefalonia: 27% / 73%
- Attica, Aegean Islands: 18.7% / 81.3%
- Crete: 15% / 85%
- Central Greece: 5.7% / 94.3%
- Epirus, Corfu Leucada: 13% / 87%
- Thrace, West Central Macedonia: 15% / 85%
- Thrace, East Macedonia: 6.7% / 93.3%
- Total: 19.2% / 80.8%

Allocation in the different areas according to the ministry of agriculture picking of their fruits are removed at the same time. About 470,000 Greek families are involved in olive cultivations in almost every geographical sector in Greece. The Peloponnese has the biggest number of trees (22,802,209), followed by the Aegean Islands (15,910,182), Crete (13,434,263), the Mainland - Euboea (12,740,281), the Ionian Islands (5,193,953), Thessaly (4,548,356), Macedonia (2,356,301), Epirus (1,683,025) and Thrace (236,677).

The average annual production of olive oil during the three-year period 1970-1972 was 205,059 tons and 60,000 tons of edible olives. The Prefecture of Lesbos is leading covering 15% of the annual production.

# Cultivation of olives - Harvesting and processing

For the olive oil to travel from the tree to your table, it has to travel through various multi-faceted and labourous processes, which begin with the proper cultivation, such as the correct choice of trees, planting, watering, weeding, fertilizing, pruning, gathering, transportation, crushing and storage.

The collecting is the greatest problem due to the absence of labour, thus oil costs in sparsely cultivated areas are high while they are lower in more densely cultivated areas. Attempts by technicians and scientists to overcome

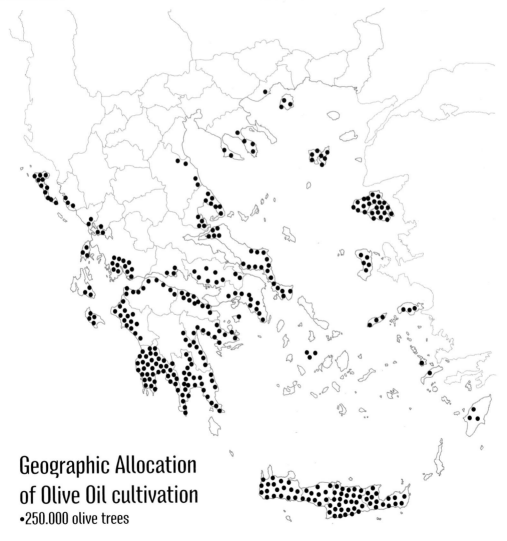

# Geographic Allocation of Olive Oil cultivation
•250.000 olive trees

# Process of olive picking and processing

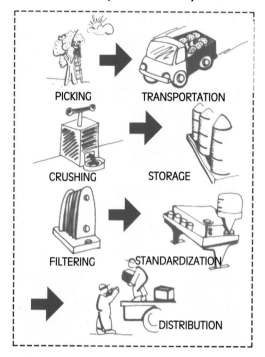

PICKING

TRANSPORTATION

CRUSHING

STORAGE

FILTERING

STANDARDIZATION

DISTRIBUTION

this problem of manual work have not yet succeeded. The olive has to undergo various procedures in order to become oil. However, the immediate picking of the olives (without them falling down), the cleanliness during the gathering process, as well as the shortest possible time from the collecting to the oil-press and the crushing process will offer the best results.

In general, it has been proved that a delay in the crushing of the fruit after being picked (together with the general condition of the fruit's cleanliness) will affect in a negative manner the quality acidity and aroma of the oil.

Transportation follows the collection process. The fruit is placed into bags, baskets or trucks in bulk form, and then transported to the oil-press. Care must be taken sogs not to damage the olives during transportation and to avoid fermentation due to lack of rentilation and increase in temperature. All these factors affect the quality of the oil. The third phase is the crushing of the olives at the oil-press. There are currently

approximately 3,500 oil-presses throughout Greece, with 5,350 presses and 51 seed-oil processing sites, from the most primitive equipment up to the most modern.

In modern mechanized oil-presses the fruit is first washed and then fed to the "crusher" where it becomes oil pulp, in order to set the oil free. It is transported to the presses or centrifuge machinery, and then channelled into the oil separators.

There are two types of oil-presses:

a) The classical type, where the final crushing takes place in the presses. There, in the first phase the virgin oil is extracted without heat and in its natural state; in the second phase the remaining oil is extracted with the added assistance of hot water. The first oil, which does not come into contact with water, is of the best quality.

b) Centrifuge or continuous operation, where the drives, after being broken, they automatically reach the separators in the form of pulp, where the oil is separated. There are pros and cons to both these systems.

The oil we have from the oil-press at this stage is natural olive oil. There are of course different qualities depending on the quality of the fruit and the method of crushing. Some oil may be used immediately as virgin oil while some -because they have increased acidity and lack of flavour, need additional processing.

There is still some oil in the residues that accumulate in the oil-presses. These stacks of residue are called oil-cake and contains some oil, depending on the efficiency of the oil-presses. This oil is known as seed-oil.

The storage, maintenance and transportation of olive oil must take place in areas and under conditions that will not alter its quality.

# Olive oil as food

Comparison of fatty substances

Olive oil is almost the only oil that is consumed in its natural state, having both aroma and flavour, in comparison to seed-oil which is tasteless and odourless.

This, together with its other attributes

and properties, separates it from the other vegetable oils (seed-oils), with respect to quality. Evaluation of its quality is carried out by expert tasters, as applies to other foodstuffs or drinks (e.g. wine, tea, coffee, etc.).

As far as to calories are concerned, all fatty substances are equal. But taking into account their nutritional value, concerning the nations of the Mediterranean, we can safely say that olive oil is superior to all other fatty substances - animal or vegetable derivatives. The superiority of olive oil is due to the following properties:

Olive oil is derived from the fruit itself while the majority of the other vegetable oils are derived from seeds. In addition, the extraction procedure utilizes crushing and not chemical solvents which carry along other dissolvable ingedients such as colouring, etc., which takes place in sunflower seed-oil and seed-oil. Therefore olive oil retains all the noble, p r o t o g e n i c ingredients of its fruit (taste, aroma, vitamins, trace elements) and is truly a biogenic food.

Olive oil has a b a l a n c e d concentration of saturated and unsaturated fatty acids, a concentration which absolutely covers the nutritional needs of the human body, as long as there is also a correct nutritional balance. With this presupposition, olive oil covers percentage-wise the qualitative and quantitative needs of the human body. In addition, it has thegreat advantage of being more stable than seed-oils are during oxidation.

Olive oil can be easily trasformed into emulsion with the effect of the gall and can be very easily digested.

# The viological value of olive oil

Up to now we have spoken about the superiority of olive oil over other animal- and vegetable-derived fatty substances, with respect to the peoples of the Mediterranean.

There is also another aspect that is just as important - its biological value. Recent scientific studies (some scientific announcements can be found at the end of the book) have added additional properties to olive oil that have labelled it as the chief healthy fatty substance.

Therefore, since it is the only oil that is derived directly from the juices of the fruit -and a fruit that has ripened under the Mediterranean sun- it preserves all the live ingredients of the fruit: taste, aroma, vitamins.

•With its aroma and especially pleasant taste, it stimulates peptic s e c r e t i o n s, mainly of bile and pancreas.

•With its chemical structure and its organ-receiving capacity, it presents the best possible indicator for digestive and absorption capacity by the intestinal walls.

•With its other properties it protects against stomach and duodenum ulcer, since it forms an emulsion layer that reduces their mobility and prevents excessive secretion of gastric juices.

•With its lubricating property it activates the intestines and suppresses atonic constipation. It has the same results with the all so common gastric disorders suffered by children, characterised by diarrhoea, and presents resistance to chemical antibiotics.

•Olive oil also acts impressively on the liver and the gall-bladder, preventing the formation of gall stones. It also causes excessive secretion of the hormone cholecystokinin which activates the gall-bladder and can be considered to be a proper medicinal.

# Scientific statements on olive oil from all over the world

In accordance with recent scientific announcements presented at the 3rd International Congress for the Biological Value of Olive Oil, held in Chania in September 1980, together with two other preceding congresses held in Lucca in Italy in October 1969 and in Malaga in Spain in May 1975, olive oil -with its wise ratio of unsaturated fatty acids, prevents the increase of cholesterol and the formation of fatty substances, increases blood-clotting properties and generally protects against arteriosclerosis

and its consequences. Specifically, professor G. Christakis G. Christakis Professor of the Department of Nutrition at the Medical School of the University of Miami stressed the following:

"Olive oil has the natural advantage of being digested and absorbed more rapidly and more completely, due to increased secretions from the bile, pancreatic amylase, lipase, as well as the secretion of cholecystokinase. Olive oil can also be used clinically for the treatment of ulcers, as proved by the reduction in size of gastric and duodenal ulcers and by its increased healing action"

M. Laval-Jeantet, a French Professor at the Laboratory for Experimental Radiology at the Saint Louis Hospital in Paris, stressed the following: "An experimental diet given to five groups of 'spraque' mice showed that edible olives which contain olive oil acids has a beneficial effect on bone development".

M. Charbonnier, a french researcher underlined the following: Olive oil has the most stimulating effect on the gall-bladder as it causes an extensive constant spasm, more effective than that of cholecystokinase when inserted intravenously"

Grawford, a French researcher at the Nuffield Laboratory for Comparative Medicine in London stated: "During pregnancy, the additional energy needs seem to be dependent on a significant amount of stored fatty substances during the early stages of pregnancy, which may later contribute towards the development of the embryo during the last stages of pregnancy, as well as dealing with partial needs during lactation. Lipids play a significant role in the development of the brain and the blood vessels"

Olive oil is also a carrier of valuable substances that cause the break-up of lipids and are: a) Carotene, a provitamin of vitamin A needed for development and health of the eye and b) Vitamin E or tocopherol, whose biological role is related to reproductive capability. This vitamin also has another property, that of antioxidation. This property makes it difficult for olive oil to oxidise, in opposition to other edible vegetable oils.

Another property is that it has a well-balanced chemical composition in fatty acids -saturated and unsaturated- and more than covers the needs of the human body without causing "lacking illnesses" or biochemical damage that arise from the use of fatty substances with excess unsaturated or saturated fatty acids. Let us not forget that the chemical composition of olive oil the closed of all to the lipid composition of maternal milk, with respect to the races of the Mediterranean.

This is the reason why in cases of premature babies that are fed with cow's milk, olive oil represents the most suitable fatty substance that would prevent certain deprivational disorders as well as covering the needs of the sensitive organism that is developing.

It also reacts decisively in arteriosclerosis and cardiac diseases. According to the results of the "Seven Countries Study" carried out in seven countries, including Greece (Mr. Aravanis as cardiologist), the people with the lowest percent of cardiovascular diseases were those living in Mediterranean countries and consumed olive oil (Greeks, Dalmations, Italians living in the south).

In general, the conclusion of the research was that a diet with lipid substances which contain unsaturated fatty acids actually decreases cholesterol levels in the blood and the formation of atheromas on the arterial walls which then develop into clots, causing coronary or myocardial attacks.

With its beneficial effect on the pancreas, olive oil is the most well-tolerated lipid for diabetics and even for persons suffering from neurofibral disorders.

Olive oil also adds vitality to the skin and hair. When Democritos was asked about the secret of longevity, he said: "Man should feed on honey and take care of his skin with oil".

Dyspepsia is not a problem with olive oil, because there is no problem of adaptability or habituation of the organism since the people of the Mediterranean have adapted since ancient times to olive oil. Every person that changes fatty substances has gastric disorders due to the organism lacking available enzymes in order to digest it. This lack will gradually disappear with the habituation.And now an important piece of information:

When lipids are cooked they change radically, especially if they are fried or roasted, and less if they are boiled with water, due to the heat temperature that is developed. The reaction from high temperatures (180-230) together with the presence of air, cause polymerism - i.e. the oxidation and formation of peroxidation, which is toxic. The new chemical compounds that are formed cause the stomach, liver, kidney and cardiovascular system damage.

In accordance with reports by the Italian Professor Viola and the Spanish Varela, olive oil -due to its large concentration of oil acids- is not altered even if fried, which may prove detrimental to the human health.

recipes in olive oil

# contents

appetisers      *19*

salads      *37*

sauses      *51*

pies      *55*

vegetables      *63*

fish - seafood      *83*

poultry - game      *105*

meat - minced meat      *111*

## OVEN TEMPERATURES

These oven temperatures are only a guide; we' ve given you the lower degree of heat. Always check the manufacturer's manual.

| | C$^0$ (Celsius) | F$^0$(Fahrenheit) | Gas Mark |
|---|---|---|---|
| Very slow | 120 | 250 | 1 |
| Slow | 150 | 300 | 2 |
| Moderately slow | 160 | 325 | 3 |
| Moderate | 180-190 | 350-375 | 4 |
| Moderately hot | 200-210 | 400-425 | 5 |
| Hot | 220-230 | 450-475 | 6 |
| Very hot | 240-250 | 500-525 | 7 |

# deteled contents

## APPETISERS

Shrimp Baked in Tomato Sauce ......................20
Pickled Baby Aubergines (Eggplant)...............20
Snail and Onion Stew .....................................21
Cheese Patties ...............................................21
Minced Meat Rolls .........................................22
Small Cheese Pies ..........................................22
Eggs, Tomatoes and Courgettes, a specialty of Crete.24
Fried Giant Beans ..........................................24
Chick Pea Fritters, a specialty of Sifnos............25
Oregano Patties.............................................25
Cod Roe Patties .............................................26
Courgette Fritters ......................................... 26
Green Peppers and Sausages, a specialty
of Pelion.......................................................27
Vine Leaves Stuffed with Rice .........................27
Salted Kalloni Sardines, a specialty of Mytilene30
Fried Peppers................................................30
Fried Courgette Flowers .................................31
Eggs and Tomatoes, a specialty of Laconia......31
Fried Courgettes (Zucchini Squash) .................32
Fried Aubergines (Eggplant) ...........................32
Tuna Salad ....................................................34
Baked Giant Beans.........................................34
Yoghurt, Cucumber and Garlic Dip.................36
Zesty Cheese Salad, a specialty of Macedonia ..36

## SALADS

Boiled Vegetable Salad....................................38
Beet Salad .....................................................38
Wild Greens Salad ..........................................39
Boiled Courgette (Zucchini Squash) Salad .......39
Cauliflower Salad............................................40
String Bean Salad ...........................................40
Lettuce Salad .................................................42
Shrimp Salad .................................................42
White Bean Salad ...........................................44
Garlic Sauce ..................................................44
Potato Salad ..................................................45
Cabbage and Carrot Salad ..............................45
Beef Salad .....................................................46
Red Cabbage Salad.........................................46
Aubergine (Eggplant) Salad ............................47
Cod Roe Salad ...............................................47
Smoked Herring Salad.....................................47
Greek Salad ...................................................50
Tomato and Cucumber Salad...........................50

# SAUSES

Mayonnaise.........................................................52
Oil and Lemon Dressing....................................52
Bechamel Sauce (for Moussakas and Pastitsio).52
Tomato Sauce with Minced Meat.....................54
Egg and Lemon Sauce .......................................54
Tomato Sauce .....................................................54

# PIES

Dough for Pie Crust ...........................................56
Onion Pie............................................................56
Courgette (Zucchini Squash) Pie .....................56
Leek Pie ..............................................................57
Spinach and Cheese Pie ....................................57
Cheese Pie ..........................................................60
Spinach Pie .........................................................60
Greens Pie ..........................................................62
Salt Cod Pie .......................................................62

# VEGETABLES (Olive oil based recipes )

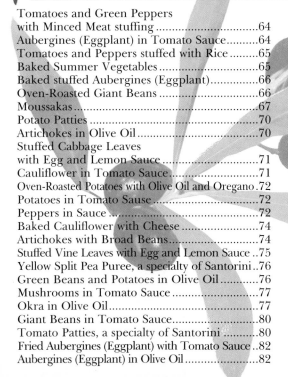

Tomatoes and Green Peppers
with Minced Meat stuffing ................................64
Aubergines (Eggplant) in Tomato Sauce..........64
Tomatoes and Peppers stuffed with Rice .........65
Baked Summer Vegetables ................................65
Baked stuffed Aubergines (Eggplant)...............66
Oven-Roasted Giant Beans ...............................66
Moussakas ..........................................................67
Potato Patties .....................................................70
Artichokes in Olive Oil.....................................70
Stuffed Cabbage Leaves
with Egg and Lemon Sauce ..............................71
Cauliflower in Tomato Sauce............................71
Oven-Roasted Potatoes with Olive Oil and Oregano .72
Potatoes in Tomato Sause .................................72
Peppers in Sauce ...............................................72
Baked Cauliflower with Cheese .......................74
Artichokes with Broad Beans...........................74
Stuffed Vine Leaves with Egg and Lemon Sauce ..75
Yellow Split Pea Puree, a specialty of Santorini ..76
Green Beans and Potatoes in Olive Oil ............76
Mushrooms in Tomato Sauce ...........................77
Okra in Olive Oil...............................................77
Giant Beans in Tomato Sauce...........................80
Tomato Patties, a specialty of Santorini ..........80
Fried Aubergines (Eggplant) with Tomato Sauce ..82
Aubergines (Eggplant) in Olive Oil..................82

# deteled contents

## FISH - SEAFOOD

Stuffed Squid ........................................................84
Stuffed Mussels, a specialty of Constantinople .84
Red Mullet in Tomato Sauce ...........................85
Grilled Lobster.....................................................85
Baked Fish ...........................................................86
Boiled Lobster .....................................................86
Fried Tope with Garlic Sauce ..........................88
Fried Whitebait.....................................................88
Whitebait in Tomato Sauce ...............................88
Lobster in Tomato Sauce ...................................89
Fried Squid ..........................................................89
Crayfish with Oil and Lemon Dressing ...........92
Baked Fresh Anchovies .....................................92
Fried Mussels.......................................................93
Grilled Fish .........................................................93
Cuttlefish with Spinach ....................................94
Shrimp with Tomato Sauce and Rice ..............94
Fish Baked in Tomato Sauce ...........................96
Boiled Fish ..........................................................96
Fried Salt Cod.....................................................97
Salt Cod in Tomato Sauce..................................97
Oven-Baked Spinach Mackerel.........................98
Pandoras in Wine ...............................................98
Shrimp with Oil and Lemon Dressing .............99
Octopus with Macaroni .....................................99
Boiled Octopus .................................................102
Octopus Stew with tiny Onions.......................102
Fried Shrimp .....................................................104
Baked Octopus, a specialty of Thessaly .........104

## POULTRY - GAME

Chicken and Noodles.......................................106
Oven-Roasted Chicken ...................................106
Chicken with Okra...........................................108
Turtle Doves with Rice ...................................108
Chicken with Lemon........................................109
Chicken in Tomato Sauce................................109
Stuffed Wild Duck...........................................110
Grilled Quail.....................................................110

Lamb Country-Style .......................................112
Veal Stew with tiny Onions ...........................112
Pork Chops with Wine ...................................113
Spit-Roasted Lamb ........................................113
Baked Lamb with Manestra ...........................116
Lamb with Artichokes....................................116
Stewed Lamb with Rice .................................118
Stuffed Lamb ................................................118
Lamb with Lemon .........................................119
Lamb with Courgettes (Zucchini Squash)......119
Fricassee of Lamb with Lettuce.....................120
Sofrito - A Specialty of Corfu .......................120
Lamb Ragout ................................................121
Lamb Offal wrapped in Intestines ................121
Oven-Roasted Lamb's Head..........................124
Stuffed Large Intestine of Mutton ................124
Roast Leg of Lamb in Paper .........................125
Lamb Liver with Olive Oil and Oregano.......125
Fried Veal Liver............................................126
Oven-Roasted Lamb .....................................126
Beef Stew with tiny Onions ..........................128
The Drinker's Appetiser.................................128
Veal with Peas...............................................129
Veal with Courgettes (Zucchini Squash).......129
Pork with White Bean ...................................130
Grilled Lamb Chops .....................................130
Kid with Oregano .........................................131
Stuffed Kid (Young Goat) .............................131
Pork with Celeriac ........................................134
Roast Leg of Pork .........................................134
Lamb in Tomato Sauce ..................................135
Garlicked Veal with Green Peppers,
a specialty of Larissa .....................................135
Grilled Meatballs...........................................136
Veal or Pork Shish Kebabs............................136
Grilled Veal Chops .......................................138
Veal with Aubergines (Eggplant) ..................138
Smyrna Meat Rolls........................................139
Fried Village Sausages...................................139
Fried Meatballs .............................................140
Meatballs in Tomato Sauce ...........................140
Stuffed Spleen...............................................141
Veal with Okra..............................................141
Veal with Macaroni.......................................142
Veal with Lemon ..........................................142
Breaded Brains..............................................143
Veal in Tomato Sauce ...................................143

# appetisers

# Garides Saganaki
## Shrimp Baked in Tomato Sauce

### SERVES 6
- 1 kg (2.2 lb) large shrimp
- 250 gr (8.8 oz) hard feta cheese
- 1 cup olive oil
- 4 ripe tomatoes or 1 tin peeled tomatoes
- 2 medium onions, finely chopped
- 1 green pepper, finely chopped
- 1 clove of garlic, finely chopped
- 1 cup parsley, finely chopped
- Salt, pepper
- Sprinkling of paprika

Peel the tomatoes, remove the seeds and put them through a food mill. Heat the oil in a pot and sauté the onion, the garlic and the green pepper. Add the tomatoes, salt and pepper. Let the sause boil for a few minutes.

Put the shrimp into an earthenware or glass baking dish and pour the sauce over them. Add the parsley, the feta, broken into pieces, add a little paprika. Bake in a hot oven for half an hour.

# Melitzanakia Toursi
## Pickled Baby Aubergines (Eggplant)

### 80-90 pieces
- 2 kg (4.4 lb) baby aubergines
- 1 large bunch parsley, finely chopped
- 2 whole garlic bulbs, peeled and finely chopped
- 2 onions, finely chopped
- 2-3 carrots, grated
- 1 kg (2.2 lb) vinegar
- 1/2 kg (1.1 lb) olive oil
- 2 table spoons salt
- Several thin stalks of celery

Wash the aubergines, cut off their stems and score them lengthwise. Place half the salt in a pot of water, bring it to a boil, and add aubergines. Boil them until they are tender but not too soft, then drain.

Mix together the parsley, garlic, onions and carrots. Stuff the aubergines with the mixture and carefully tie them shut with the celery stalks. Put the aubergines into a glazed earthenware container with the oil, vinegar and the rest of the salt. Leave them in a cool, dark place for 15 days.

# Salingaria Stifado
## Snail and Onion Stew

### SERVES 5
- I kg (2.2 lb) medium snails
- 1 kg (2.2 lb) onions, sliced and separated into rings
- 1 cup olive oil
- 2 cloves garlic, finely chopped
- 2 tablespoons vinegar
- 2 bay leaves
- A little fresh rosemary
- 5 ripe tomatoes, peeled and finely chopped
- Salt, pepper

The evening before cooking, put the snails in a bowl of water and cover it with a plate to keep them from crawling away. Wash them well, keeping only the live ones. Boil them for 15 minutes. With the point of a knife, make a hole in the rear side of each shell. Rinse them well and drain.

Heat the olive oil in a pot and brown the onions and garlic. Add the tomatoes, bay leaves, vinegar, rosemary, salt, pepper and a little water and let the sauce boil for about 15 minutes. Add the snails and continue cooking for another 20-30 minutes until most of the water has evaporated and the sauce has thickened.

# Tirokeftedakia
## Cheese Patties

### SERVES 8
- 250 gr (8.8 oz) kefalotiri cheese
- 2 eggs beaten
- A little parsley, finely chopped
- Pepper
- Olive oil or butter for frying
- 1/2 cup rusk crumbs

Grate the cheese coarsely. Beat the eggs well, add the rest of the ingredients except the oil, and mix together. If the mixture is not firm enough, add some more crumbs. Shape into patties and fry in oil or butter.

# Bourekakia me Kima
## Minced Meat Rolls

### SERVES 10
- 500 gr (17.7 oz) minced meat
- 500 gr (17.7 oz) phyllo dough
- 1 large onion, finely chopped
- 2 tablespoons rusk crumbs
- Juice of 2 tomatoes
- 1 cup kefalotiri cheese, grated
- 1 cup butter or margarine
- 1 egg
- 1 bay leaf
- Salt, pepper
- Parsley, finely chopped

Sauté the onion lightly in the butter and add the minced meat. Continue to sauté, stirring continually. Add the salt, pepper, tomato juice and bay leaf. Reduce the heat and cook the meat for approximately 30 minutes longer, until all the liquid has evaporated. Add the beaten egg, the cheese, the crumbs and the parsley.
Cut the phyllo dough into strips, brush each one with butter, and place one spoonful of the mixture on each strip. Roll them up to form small cylinders, place them on a buttered baking sheet and brush them with the remaining butter. Bake in a moderate oven for 20-25 minutes.

# Tiropitakia
## Small Cheese Pies

### SERVES 8-10
- 250 gr (8.8 oz) hard feta cheese
- 10 sheets of phyllo dough
- 1 cup melted butter
- 2 eggs beaten
- A little mint, finely chopped
- Pinch of pepper

Mash the cheese with a fork and add the beaten eggs, the mint and the pepper. Cut the phyllo dough into strips 6 cm (2.4 inches) wide. Brush each strip with butter, place a teaspoonful of the filling on one end and fold it up into a triangle. Put the cheese pies onto a buttered baking sheet, brush them with a little melted butter and bake in a moderate oven 15-20 minutes until golden brown.

# Sfoungato
## Eggs, Tomatoes and Courgettes, a Specialty of Crete

**SERVES 4**
- 500 gr (17.6 oz) courgettes (zucchini squash)
- 500 gr (17.6 oz) ripe tomatoes
- 2 medium onions, **finely** chopped
- 5 eggs
- 1/2 cup olive oil
- Salt, pepper

Peel the tomatoes, remove the seeds and chop them up fine, Heat the oil in a frying pan and brown the onions with the courgettes cut into round slices. Add the chopped tomatoes, salt and pepper. Cook until most of the liquid has evaporated and add the well-beaten eggs. Simmer for a few minutes. Serve hot or cold.

# Gigantes Tiganiti
## Fried Giant Beans

**SERVES 6-7**
- 500 gr (17.6 oz) giant dried white beans
- 1 cup flour
- 2 eggs
- 2 tablespoons milk
- 1 cup rusk crumbs
- Salt, pepper
- Parsley, finely chopped
- Olive oil for frying

The night before cooking, put the beans in water to soak. Next day drain them and boil them in plenty of water, until they are tender, but still firm. In one bowl, place the flour mixed with the salt and pepper, in another the beaten eggs, and in a third the rusk crumbs.
Heat the oil in a frying pan. Dip each bean first in the flour, then in the egg and finally in the rusk crumbs, before frying. Garnish with finely chopped parsley and serve at once.

# Revithokeftedes
## Chick Pea Fritters, a Specialty of Sifnos

**SERVES 6-7**
- 500 gr (17.6 oz) dried chick peas
- 2 teaspoons baking soda
- 2 medium onions, finely chopped
- 1 small bunch parsley, finely chopped
- 1 egg
- 1 cup flour
- Salt, pepper
- Olive oil for frying

Soak the chick peas in warm water with the baking soda for 12-14 hours. Drain and wash them well and put them through a food mill or purée them in a mixer. Add the onions, parsley, egg, salt and pepper. Mix well and shape the mixture into patties. Dredge the patties in flour and fry them in hot oil.

# Riganokeftedes
## Oregano Patties

**SERVES 8-10**
- 1 kg (2.2 lb) potatoes
- 125 gr (4.4 oz) salted cod roe
- 1 large onion, finely chopped
- 2 eggs, beaten
- 1 level tablespoon oregano
- Crumbs of 2 rusks
- Pepper
- 1 cup flour
- Olive oil for frying

Boil the potatoes whole, remove the skins and, while still warm, put them through a food mill or purée them using a mixer. Add the remaining ingredients, except the flour and the oil. Mix well, and leave the mixture in the refrigerator until firm. Form into patties, dredge them in flour and fry them in hot oil.

# Taramokeftedes
## Cod Roe Patties

### SERVES 8
- 150 gr (5.3 oz) salted cod roe
- 200 gr (7 oz) crustless bread, soaked in water
- 3 tablespoons flour
- Half a bunch of dillweed
- Half a bunch of parsley
- A little fresh mint
- 3 spring onions
- 1 cup flour
- Olive oil for frying

Chop the herbs and onions fine. Knead them together with the bread, from which the excess water has been pressed, the roe and 3 tablespoons of flour, to form a rather firm mixture. Shape into patties, dredge them in flour and fry them in hot oil.

# Kolokithokeftedes
## Courgette Fritters

### SERVES 8
- 1 kg (2.2 lb) courgettes (zucchini squash)
- 250 gr (8.8 oz) grated feta cheese
- 2 eggs, beaten
- 1 cup rusk crumbs
- Parsley, finely chopped
- 1 cup flour
- Salt, pepper
- Olive oil for frying

Scrape the outsides of the courgettes. Wash and grate them fine. Put them into a colander, add salt and let them drain for about an hour. Squeeze as much liquid as possible out of them. Put the courgette pulp into a bowl, add the feta cheese, eggs, crumbs, parsley and pepper, and knead the mixture. If it is not firm enough add a few more rusk crumbs or a little flour. Shape into patties, dredge them in flour and fry them in hot oil.

# Dolmadakia Yalantzi
## Vine Leaves Stuffed with Rice

### SERVES 4
- 250 gr (8.8 oz) grapevine leaves
- 500 gr (17.6 oz) spring onions, finely chopped
- 1 cup olive oil
- 1 cup rice
- 1 small bunch dillweed, finely chopped
- 1 small bunch mint, finely chopped
- Juice of 1 lemon

Blanch the leaves, rinse with cold water and drain, Sauté the spring onions for a few minutes in half the oil. Add the rice, 1 cup hot water and the rest of the ingredients, except the oil and lemon juice. Boil the mixture for 4-5 minutes.

Roll up a teaspoonful of the mixture in each leaf. Place the vine leaf rolls in a pot in firmly packed layers consisting of concentric circles. Cover them with a plate and add the rest of the oil, the lemon juice and 2 cups of water. Cook them over low heat for about half an hour, until the water has been absorbed and the rice is tender. Serve cold, garnished with lemon slices.

# Spetsofai
## Green Peppers and Sausages, a Specialty of Pelion

### SERVES 6
- 1 kg (2.2 lb) green peppers
- 4 village-made sausages
- 1 kg tomatoes
- 2 medium onions, finely chopped
- 1 cup olive oil
- Salt, pepper
- Pinch of sugar

Put the tomatoes through a food mill. Cut the peppers and sausages into slices, heat the oil and sauté them lightly. Add the remaining ingredients and simmer until the sauce has thickened.

# Sardeles Kallonis Pastes
## Salted Kalloni Sardines, a Specialty of Mytilene

- *2 kg (4.4 lb) small sardines*
- Pickling salt
- Olive oil
- Vinegar

Remove the intestines from the sardines, wash and drain them well. In a glazed earthenware or glass container, alternate layers of salt and fish, beginning and ending with a layer of salt. Put a weight on the top and let stand for a month. Take out sardines as needed, wash them well and serve them with olive oil and vinegar.

# Piperies  Tiganites
## Fried  Peppers

### SERVES 6

- 500 gr (17.6 oz) sweet yellow peppers (long, tapered type)
- Olive oil for frying
- A little vinegar
- Salt

Wash the peppers well, pat them dry and prick them with a fork. Heat the oil in a frying pan and fry the peppers, taking care they do not get too brown. Take them out of the frying pan and sprinkle with salt and vinegar.

# Kolokithoanthi Tiganiti
## Fried Courgette Flowers

### SERVES 5
- 15 courgette flowers
- 1/2 cup flour
- 1 egg, beaten
- 1/2 cup milk
- 1 tablespoon olive oil
- Salt
- Olive oil for frying

Wash the courgette flowers and remove the small green leaves. Make a thick batter with the flour, egg, milk, the tablespoon of oil and the salt.
Dip the flowers one by one into the batter and fry them in hot oil.

# Kayanos
## Eggs and Tomatoes, a Specialty of Laconia

### SERVES 3
- 500 gr (17.6 oz) ripe tomatoes
- 6 eggs, beaten
- Salt, pepper
- 1/2 cup olive oil

Peel the tomatoes, remove the seeds and rub them through a coarse grater. Put them into a frying pan and boil until most of their juice has evaporated.
In another frying pan, heat the oil, pour in the tomatoes and sauté them for a few minutes. Add the beaten eggs, salt and pepper and stir until thick.
Variation: Just before the kayanos is done, add grated feta cheese and stir.

# Kolokithakia Tiganita
## Fried Courgettes (Zucchini Squash)

### SERVES 8
• 1 kg (2.2 lb) large courgettes
• 1 cup flour
• Salt, pepper
• Olive oil for frying

Wash the courgettes and cut them into thin slices. Mix the flour with the salt and pepper. Dredge the courgettes in the mixture. Heat the oil in a frying pan and fry the courgettes until golden brown. Serve at once.

# Melitzanes Tiganites
## Fried Aubergines (Eggplant)

### SERVES 8
• 1 kg (2.2 lb) aubergines
• 1 cup flour
• Salt, pepper
• Olive oil for frying

Wash the aubergines and cut them into slices. Salt them and leave them to drain in a colander for about an hour. Rinse them and squeeze out the excess liquid. Mix the flour with the pepper. Dredge the aubergines in the flour and fry them in hot oil. Serve at once.

## Tonossalata
### Tuna Salad

**SERVES 4**
- 1 tin of tuna
- 1 small onion, finely chopped
- Olive oil
- Lemon juice
- A little mustard
- Pinch of salt
- Parsley, finely chopped

Mix the oil, lemon juice, mustard and salt. Crush the tuna with a fork, add the onion and oil and lemon mixture and mix together. Garnish with the finely chopped parsley.

## Gigantes Plaki
### Bake Giant Beans

**SERVES 6**
- 500 gr (17.6 oz) giant dried white beans
- 1 large onion, sliced and separated into rings
- 2-3 cloves of garlic
- 4 ripe tomatoes
- 1 scant cup olive oil
- Salt, pepper
- 1 bunch parsley, finely chopped

Put the beans in water to soak 12 hours before cooking. Drain and boil them in plenty of water. Drain again and put them in an earthenware baking dish. Peel the tomatoes, remove the seeds, put them through a food mill and pour them into the baking dish with the beans. Add the remaining ingredients, stir and bake in a moderate oven for about one hour. If necessary, add a little water during cooking.

# Tzatziki
## Yoghurt, Cucumber and Garlic Dip

**SERVES 6**
- 2 cups strained full-fat yoghurt
- 1 medium cucumber
- 4 cloves of garlic, mashed to a paste
- 2 tablespoons olive oil
- Salt
- Pinch of pepper
- A little vinegar
- Fresh dillweed, finely chopped
- A few ripe olives

Grate the peeled cucumber on a coarse grater and press as much liquid as possible out of it. Mix the cucumber with the rest of the ingredients. Garnish with the olives.

# Tirossalata Kafteri
## Zesty Cheese Salad, a Specialty of Macedonia

**SERVES 4**
- 200 gr (7 oz) feta cheese
- 1 long hot pepper
- 3-4 tablespoons olive oil
- A little vinegar

Cook the pepper under the grill. Remove the skin and seeds and cut it into small pieces. Mash the feta cheese with a fork. Put all the ingredients into the blender or blend with a mortar and pestle until they are the consistency of paste. Variation: Use soft mizithra cheese instead of feta.

# salads

# Salata me Vrasta Lahanika
## Boiled Vegetable Salad

### SERVES 6
• 250 gr (8.8 oz) courgettes (zucchini squash)
• 250 gr (8.8 oz) green beans
• 500 gr (17.6 oz) potatoes
• 150 gr (5.3 oz) carrots
• 250 gr (8.8 oz) beetroot
• Oil and lemon dressing
• Salt
• Parsley, finely chopped

Boil the vegetables, cut them in small pieces and salt them. Place them in layers in a salad bowl. Dress with oil and lemon and garnish with finely chopped parsley.

# Patzaria Salata
## Beet Salad

### SERVES 6
• 1 kg (2.2 lb) beets
• Olive oil
• Vinegar
• Salt
• 2 cloves of garlic, finely chopped

Clean and wash the beets and separate the roots from the leaves. Boil the roots first, in salted water, for half an hour. Add the leaves and boil 20 minutes longer. Drain, peel the roots and cut them into slices. Place the beetroot, the leaves and the finely chopped garlic in a salad bowl and dress with oil and vinegar.
Variation: Garlic sauce (skordalia) may be used instead of oil and vinegar.

# Horta Vounou Salata
## Wild Greens Salad

### SERVES 4

• 1 kg (2.2 lb) various wild greens
• Salt
• Oil and lemon dressing

Pick and wash the greens. Put them in a pot of boiling water and boil for about 30 minutes without covering the pot. Drain, salt and serve dressed with oil and lemon.

# Kolokithakia Vrasta Salata
## Boiled Courgette (Zucchini Squash) Salad

### SERVES 5

• 1 kg (2.2 lb) medium courgettes
• Salt
• 6 tablespoons olive oil
• Juice of 1/2 lemon

Bring a pot of salted water to a boil and add the courgettes, which have been cleaned and washed. Boil for about 15 minutes. Slice the courgettes and pour the oil and lemon dressing over them.

# Kounoupidi Salata
## Cauliflower Salad

### SERVES 5-6
- 1 large cauliflower
- 1/2 cup olive oil
- Juice of 1 lemon
- Salt
- A little oregano (optional)

Remove any tough stems from the cauliflower and wash it. Bring a pot of salted water to a boil and add the cauliflower. Let it boil for about 25 minutes. Serve the cauliflower dressed with oil and lemon and a sprinkling of oregano.
Note: Broccoli salad may be made in the same way.

# Ambelofassoula Salata
## String Bean Salad

### SERVES 4
- 1 kg (2.2 lb) string beans
- 6 tablespoons olive oil
- 1 tablespoon vinegar
- Salt

Clean and wash the string beans. Boil them in salted water for 20 minutes in an open pot. Dress with oil and vinegar.
Variation: The oil and vinegar may be replaced with garlic sauce (see 16. Garlic Sauce - Skordalia).

# Maroulossalata
## Lettuce Salad

### SERVES 4
• 1 large head of lettuce
• 4-5 spring onions, finely chopped
• Salt
• Oil and vinegar dressing or oil and lemon dressing
• Fresh dill weed, finely chopped

Clean and wash the lettuce. Pat the leaves dry and cut them into thin strips. Add the onions and dillweed to the lettuce. Salt the salad and dress with oil and vinegar or oil and lemon.

# Garidosalata
## Shrimp Salad

### SERVES 6
• 1 kg (2.2 lb) shrimp
• 3 potatoes, boiled but not too soft
• 2 tablespoons pickled cucumbers, sliced
• 2 tablespoons capers
• Salt, pepper
• Parsley, finely chopped
• Vinegar

Boil the shrimp in salted water, to which a little vinegar has been added. Peel and devein the shrimp, cut the potatoes into cubes, and place them in a salad bowl, along with the pickled cucumber and the capers. Stir to mix. Beat the oil and lemon dressing and pour it over the salad. Garnish with finely chopped parsley.

# Fassolia Xera Salata
## White Bean Salad

### SERVES 6
• 500 gr (17.6 oz) white beans
• 1 medium onion, finely chopped
• Oil and lemon dressing
• Parsley, finely chopped
• Salt

Put the beans in water to soak 12 hours before preparation time. Drain the beans, place in a pot of water and boil until tender. Drain again and put them in a salad bowl. Add salt and the chopped onion, dress with oil and lemon and garnish with finely chopped parsley.

# Skordalia
## Garlic Sauce

• 5-6 cloves of garlic
• 150 gr (5.3 oz) boiled potatoes
• 1/2 cup olive oil
• A little vinegar
• Salt

Peel and mash the garlic to a paste. Add the potatoes and mash. Add 1-2 teaspoons vinegar and dribble in the oil, mixing constantly. Serve the skordalia garnished with olives.
Variations: 1. A little lemon may be added along with the olive oil.
2. The potatoes may be replaced with crustless bread, which has been soaked in water and squeezed.

# Patatossalata
## Potato Salad

### SERVES 6
- 1 kg (2.2 lb) potatoes
- 1 onion, sliced
- Juice of one lemon
- 1/2 cup olive oil
- Salt, pepper
- Parsley, finely chopped
- A few ripe olives, pickled in vinegar

Boil the potatoes whole in salted water. Peel, slice and place them in a salad bowl. Add the rest of the ingredients and stir well.

Variations 1: The parsley may be replaced with oregano, and finely chopped pickled cucumbers can be added.

2. Add a little garlic, pounded to a paste, to the oil and lemon dressing.

# Salata me Lahano kai Karota
## Cabbage and Carrot Salad

### SERVES 8
- 1 small firm head of cabbage
- 3 carrots
- 1/2 cup olive oil
- Lemon juice
- Salt

Shred and salt the cabbage and place it in a colander to wilt for 1/2 -1 hour. Rinse it well and put it in a salad bowl. Clean, wash and grate the carrots and mix them in with the cabbage. Dress the salad with oil and lemon.

Note: Prepare the oil and lemon dressing without salt, as the cabbage has already been salted.

Variation: Make the oil and lemon dressing using the juice of only 1/2 lemon and add a clove of garlic, crushed, and a little mustard.

# Vodino Salata
## Beef Salad

### a. For the boiled beef:
- 1 kg (2.2 lb) brisket of beef
- 2 stalks celery
- A little parsley
- 1 bay leaf
- 1 onion
- 1 carrot
- Whole peppercorns
- Salt

### b. For the salad:
- 3 medium potatoes, boiled and sliced
- 250 gr (8.8 oz) green beans, boiled
- 1 medium onion, sliced
- 2 medium tomatoes, sliced
- Pickled cucumbers
- Parsley, finely chopped

### c. For the oil and lemon  dressing:
- 1/2 cup olive oil
- Juice of 1 lemon
- 1/2 teaspoon mustard
- Salt, pepper

Bring plenty of water to a boil in a pot and add the salt and the meat, cut into serving pieces. Skim off the foam, add the remaining ingredients for the boiled beef, cover the pot and let simmer for 2 - 2 1/2 hours.
Place the salad ingredients and the meat, cut into small pieces, in  a salad bowl. Beat the dressing ingredients well and pour the dressing over the salad. Stir and garnish with finely chopped parsley.

# Kokino Lahano Salata
## Red Cabbage Salad

### SERVES 6
- 1 head red cabbage
- Oil and lemon dressing
- Salt

Shred the cabbage and wash it well. Place it in a salad bowl, add salt, and dress with oil and lemon.

# Melitzanossalata
## Aubergine (Eggplant) Salad

### SERVES 6
- 1 kg (2.2 lb) large purple aubergines
- 1 cup olive oil
- Juice of 1 lemon
- 2 cloves of garlic, mashed to a paste
- Salt

Prick the aubergines with a fork and bake them in the oven. Peel them and beat them in a blender with the lemon and the salt. Continue to blend, adding the garlic and olive oil a little at a time.

# Taramossalata
## Cod Roe Salad

### SERVES 4- 5
- 100 gr (3.5 oz) salted cod roe
- 300 gr boiled potatoes
- 1 cup olive oil
- 1 small onion, grated
- Juice of 1 1/2 lemons

Mash the roe, potatoes and onion until smooth. Add the oil and lemon juice in turns, little by little. Garnish with olives and the heart of a lettuce or with finely chopped parsley.
Variation: Soaked and squeezed crustless bread may be substituted for the potatoes.

# Rengossalata
## Smoked herring Salad

### SERVES 6
- 500 gr (17.6 oz) boiled potatoes
- 1 large onion
- 1 large carrot
- 2 smoked herring
- Oil and lemon dressing

Slice the onion thinly. Clean and grate the carrot. Cut the potato into small cubes. Clean the herring and remove the bones, cut them in small pieces and put them in a salad bowl. Add the onion, carrot and potatoes. Mix together and dress with oil and lemon.

# Horiatiki Salata
## Greek Salad

### SERVES 6
• 4 firm ripe tomatoes
• 1 cucumber
• 1 medium onion
• 1 green pepper
• 150 gr (5.1 oz) feta cheese
• A few ripe olives
• A few capers
• 1/2 cup olive oil
• Sprinkling of oregano
• Salt

Wash the tomatoes, peel the cucumber and cut into slices. Cut the onion and pepper in rings. Place them in a salad bowl, add the olives, capers, oregano and salt, and mix lightly. Slice the feta cheese, place it on top of the salad and dress with olive oil.

# Angourodomatossalata
## Tomato and Cucumber Salad

### SERVES 4
• 1 medium cucumber
• 3 tomatoes, ripe but firm
• 5 tablespoons olive oil
• Salt
• Oregano (optional)

Wash the tomatoes and peel the cucumber, slice and place in a salad bowl. Sprinkle on the oregano and salt, and dress the salad with the olive oil.

# sauces

# Mayoneza
## Mayonnaise

• 1 cup olive oil
• 2 egg yolks
• 1 tablespoon lemon juice
• 1 tablespoon vinegar
• Pinch of sugar
• 1 teaspoon mustard
• Pinch of salt
• A littler white pepper

Beat the eggs, sugar, mustard, salt, pepper and vinegar. Continue to beat, adding the oil a few drops at a time. While still beating, add the lemon juice, a few drops at a time.

# Bessamel
## Bechamel Sauce (for Moussakas and Pastitsio)

• 4 cups hot milk
• 8 tablespoons flour
• 3 tablespoons butter or margarine
• Salt, pepper
• Pinch of nutmeg

Melt the butter in a small pot, add the flour and stir well with a wooden spoon. Turn the heat down very low and add the hot milk, little by little, stirring constantly to keep the flour from forming lumps. Let the sauce thicken, stirring continually. Add the salt, pepper and the nutmeg.
Variations: 1. When the sauce has thickened, remove it from the heat and gradually stir in two beaten eggs.
2. If the Bechamel sauce is to be used for pastitsio, stir in 1/2-1 cup grated cheese (kasseri or kefalotiri) at the end.

# Ladolemono
## Oil and Lemon Dressing

• 1/2 cup olive oil
• Juice of 1 lemon
• Salt, pepper

Put the ingredients in a glass jar, screw on the lid and shake. This is a dressing for fish or salads.
Variations: 1. Add oregano, finely chopped parsley or finely chopped onion to the oil and lemon.
2. Add 1/2 teaspoon mustard to the oil and lemon.

# Saltsa Domatas me Kima
## Tomato Sauce with Minced Meat

- 500 gr (17.6 oz) minced meat
- 4 ripe tomatoes or 1 tin peeled tomatoes
- 2 tablespoons oil
- 1 large onion, finely chopped
- 1 demitasse cup red wine
- 1 bay leaf
- Parsley, finely chopped

Heat the oil in a pot and sauté the onion lightly. Add the minced meat, sauté for a few minutes longer and pour in the wine. Add the tomatoes, peeled and chopped, the bay leaf and the salt and pepper. Simmer the sauce for about 40 minutes. Ten minutes before cooking time is up, add the parsley.
Variation: Add a little stick cinnamon and 1-2 cloves to the sauce.

# Avgolemono
## Egg and Lemon Sauce

- 1 - 2  cups broth from soup or liquid from entree
- 2 eggs
- Juice of 1 lemon
- A little flour

Mix the flour with the lemon juice. Beat the eggs in a bowl with the flour and lemon juice. Add the broth or other liquid little by little, beating continually. Pour the egg and lemon sauce into the pot of soup or food and stir.
Note: Remove the pot from the heat before adding the egg and lemon sauce.
Variation: If a thinner sauce is desired, you may omit the flour.

# Saltsa Domatas
## Tomato Sauce

- Oil
- 1 kg (2.2 lb) ripe tomatoes
- 1 large onion, finely chopped
- Pinch of sugar
- 1 carrot, grated
- A little celery, finely chopped
- Salt, pepper

Heat the oil in a pot and sauté the onion, carrot and celery. Add the tomatoes, which have been peeled and chopped, along with the salt, pepper and sugar. Simmer the sauce for about 40 minutes. Put it through a food mill and bring it to a boil again for 2-3 minutes. The sauce accompanies pasta or rice.

# pies

# Zimi gia Filo Pitas
## Dough for Pie Crust

**SERVES 4**
- 500 gr (17.6 oz) flour
- 1 demitasse cup olive oil
- 1 cup lukewarm water
- 1 level teaspoon salt

Reserve a little flour for rolling out the dough. Put the rest of the flour into a basin, make a well in the middle and place the water, salt and oil in it. Knead to form a soft dough and separate it into balls (one for each crust). Roll out the dough on a floured surface.

# Kremidopita
## Onion Pie

- 500 gr (17.6 oz) hard feta cheese
- 500 gr (17.6 oz) spring onions, finely chopped
- 1 small bunch dillweed, finely chopped
- 3 eggs, beaten
- Pepper
- 1/2 cup olive oil
- 2 thick pie crusts
- Melted butter

Mash the feta cheese with a fork. Add the eggs, pepper, onions, dillweed and olive oil and blend well. Line a oiled baking pan with one of the crusts, spread the filling over it and cover with the other crust. Brush the top crust with butter and bake in a moderate oven for half an hour. Variation: Substitute 250 gr (8.8 oz) fresh mizithra or anthotiro cheese for half the feta.

# Kolokithopita
## Courgette (Zucchini Squash) Pie

- 1 kg (2.2 lb) courgettes
- 1 onion, finely chopped
- 200 gr (7 oz) feta cheese, broken in small pieces
- 1 cup grated cheese
- 3 eggs, beaten
- 2 tablespoons rusk crumbs
- 1 cup olive oil
- Pepper
- Pinch of salt
- 500 gr (17.6 oz) phyllo dough
- Olive oil for the baking pan and phyllo sheets

Wash the courgettes and grate them. Place them in a pot with the onion and boil until most of the liquid has evaporated. Mix them with the rest of the ingredients. Put half the phyllo dough in an oiled baking pan, brushing each sheet with oil before adding the next. Spread the filling over these and cover with the remaining sheets of dough, again oiling each one. Bake the courgette pie in a moderate oven for approximately 45 minutes.

## Prassopita
### Leek Pie

• 1 kg (2.2 lb) leeks
• 2 eggs
• 300 gr (10.6 oz) hard feta cheese
• Salt , pepper
•  500 gr (17.6 oz) phyllo dough

Cut off and discard the green parts of the leeks. Wash the white parts, chop them fine and boil them in a little water. Drain, press out excess water and add the beaten eggs, the feta cheese, mashed with a fork, half the olive oil, the salt and pepper, and stir well. Brush a baking pan with oil and line it with half the phyllo sheets, oiling each one as it is added. Add the filling and cover the pie with the remaining sheets, oiling them one by one. Bake the leek pie in a moderate oven for approximately one hour.

## Spanakotiropita
### Spinach and Cheese Pie

• 1 kg (2.2 lb) fresh spinach
• 250 gr (8.8 oz) feta cheese
• 1 large leek, finely chopped
• 300 gr (10.6 oz) spring onions, finely chopped
• 1 1/2 cup olive oil
• 1/2 bunch dillweed, finely chopped
• 1/2 bunch parsley, finely chopped
• 2 eggs
• Salt, pepper
• 500 gr (17.6 oz) phyllo dough

Pick, wash and blanch the spinach. Chop it after squeezing out all excess liquid. Mash the feta cheese with a fork. Heat half the oil and sauté the onions and leek lightly. Remove the pot from the heat, add the dillweed, parsley, feta cheese, beaten eggs, spinach, salt and pepper, and stir to mix. Brush a baking pan with oil, and line it with half the sheets of phyllo dough, brushing each one with oil as it is added. Put in the filling and cover the pie with the rest of the  dough, oiling it as before. Bake the spinach and cheese pie in a moderate oven for one hour.
Variation: Add 1/2 cup evaporated milk or fresh cream to the filling.

57

# Spanakopita
## Spinach Pie

- 1 kg (2.2 lb) fresh spinach
- 300 gr (10.6 oz) spring onions, finely chopped
- 1 small bunch dillweed, finely chopped
- 1 large leek, finely chopped
- 2 eggs
- 1 cup olive oil
- Salt, pepper
- 500 gr (17.6 oz) phyllo dough

Pick, wash and blanch the spinach. Press out all excess liquid and chop it. Heat half the oil and sauté the onions and leek lightly. Remove the pot from the heat, add the dillweed, the beaten eggs, the spinach, the salt and pepper and stir to mix. Brush a baking pan with oil and line it with half the phyllo dough, brushing the sheets one by one. Add the filling and cover the pie with the remaining phyllo dough, oiling each sheet as before. Bake the spinach pie in a moderate oven for one hour.

# Tiropita
## Cheese Pie

- 500 gr (17.6 oz) feta cheese
- 100 gr (3.5 oz) kefalograviera cheese, grated
- 1 cup milk
- 1/2 cup olive oil
- Dillweed or mint, finely chopped
- 4 eggs, beaten
- Pepper
- Olive oil to grease the sheets of dough
- 500 gr (17.6 oz) of phyllo dough

Mash the feta cheese with a fork. Add the kefalograviera cheese, the milk, oil, dillweed or mint, eggs and pepper. Oil a baking pan and line it with half the phyllo dough, brushing each sheet with oil as it is added. Spread the cheese mixture over this and cover with the rest of the dough, oiling in the same way. Bake the cheese pie in a moderate oven for about an hour.

# Xortopita
## Greens Pie

- 1 1/2 kg (3.3 lb) various tender greens
- 3- 4 spring onions
- 250 gr (8.8 oz) feta cheese
- 1 1/2 cup olive oil
- Dillweed and parsley, finely chopped
- 4 beaten eggs
- 2 tablespoons rusk crumbs
- Pinch of salt and pepper
- 500 gr (17.6 oz) phyllo dough

Pick, wash and blanch the greens, squeeze out the excess liquid and chop them. Mash the feta cheese with a fork. Heat half the oil and sauté the onions and greens. Remove the pot from the heat and add the cheese, eggs, dillweed, parsley, crumbs, salt and pepper. Oil a baking pan and line it with half the phyllo dough, brushing each sheet with oil as it is added. Add the filling and cover the pie with the rest of the  dough, oiling in the same way. Bake the greens pie in a moderate oven for approximately one hour.

# Bakaliaropita
## Salt Cod Pie

- 800 gr (1 3/4 lb) salt cod
- 1 cup olive oil
- 2 onions, finely chopped
- 150 gr (5.3 oz) rice
- 2 small ripe tomatoes
- 2 cloves garlic, finely chopped
- Parsley, finely chopped
- Pepper
- 2 pie crusts (not too thin)

Put the cod in water to soak the day before cooking, changing the water several times. It must soak for at least 18 hours. Remove the bones and skin and cut the cod into small pieces. Peel the tomatoes, remove the seeds and chop them. Reserve a little oil for oiling the crusts and the pan, and heat the rest in a pot. Brown the onion and add the remaining ingredients, except the rice and pie crusts. Stir for a few minutes over medium heat, add the rice and cook for 1-2 minutes longer. Line an oiled baking pan with one of the crusts and fill it with the cod mixture. Cover with the second crust and brush the top with oil. Bake the pie in a moderate oven for one hour or so until the top crust is golden brown.
Note: The recipe does not call for salt because the cod is already salty. You may test the filling for salt before filling the pie and add some if necessary.

# vegetables

# Gemista me Kima

## Tomatoes and Green Peppers with Minced Meat Stuffing

### SERVES 6

• 6 medium tomatoes
• 6 medium green peppers
• 1 1/2 cup olive oil
• 1 medium onion, finely chopped
• 500 gr (17.6 oz) minced beef
• 1/2 cup rice
• Parsley, finely chopped
• Salt, pepper
• Rusk crumbs
• 2 cups tomato juice

Wash the tomatoes and peppers. Cut a thin slice off the stem-ends and hollow out the interiors. Keep the tomato pulp, and chop it up or purée it in the blender. Heat 1/2 cup olive oil and sauté the onion and minced meat. Add the tomato pulp, rice, parsley, salt and pepper and simmer. Stuff the tomatoes and peppers, put their lids back on and arrange them in a baking pan. Pour the rest of the oil and the tomato juice over them and sprinkle them with the rusk crumbs. Bake in a moderate oven for approximately 1 hour.

# Melitzanes Imam Baildi

## Aubergines (Eggplant) in Tomato Sauce

### SERVES 5-6

• 1 1/2 kg (3.3 lb) aubergines (long, narrow type)
• Olive oil for frying
• 6 ripe tomatoes
• 1/2 cup olive oil
• 6 cloves garlic, finely chopped
• 500 gr (17.6 oz) onions, thinly sliced
• Salt, pepper
• Parsley, finely chopped
•Pinch of sugar

Clean and wash the aubergines and make cross-shaped incisions on them. Lightly fry the aubergines uncut. Heat the oil in a pot and sauté the onions. Add the tomatoes, peeled and put through a food mill, the garlic, parsley, sugar, salt and pepper, and cook for 10 minutes. Stuff the aubergines with the onion mixture. Place them in an ovenproof glass dish and pour the remaining sauce over them, adding a little water. Bake them in a moderate oven for approximately one hour. This is a dish usually served cold.

# Gemista Ladera
## Tomatoes and Peppers Stuffed with Rice

### SERVES 6
- 7 medium tomatoes
- 6 medium green peppers
- 1 1/2 cup rice
- 2 medium onions, finely chopped
- Parsley, finely chopped
- 1 1/2 cup olive oil
- Salt, pepper
- Rusk crumbs
- 2 cups tomato juice

Wash the tomatoes and peppers. Cut a thin slice off the stem-ends and hollow out the interiors. Keep the tomato pulp, and chop it up or purée it in the blender. Mix the rice, onion, parsley, tomato pulp, 1/2 cup olive oil,  salt and pepper. Fill the tomatoes and peppers with the mixture, cover them with the lids you have sliced off and arrange them in a baking pan. Pour the tomato juice and the rest of the oil over them and sprinkle the lids with rusk crumbs. Bake them in a moderate oven for 1-1 1/2 hours.

# Briam Fournou
## Baked Summer Vegetables

### SERVES 6 - 8
- 1 kg (2.2 lb) courgettes (zucchini squash)
- 1 kg (2.2 lb) potatoes
- 1 kg (2.2 lb) aubergines (eggplant)
- 3 onions, sliced
- 2 green peppers, cut in thin slices
- 1 kg (2.2 lb) ripe peeled tomatoes or 1 tin peeled tomatoes
- Salt, pepper
- 1 bunch parsley, finely chopped
- 1 cup olive oil

Clean and wash the courgettes, aubergines and potatoes. Cut them in slices. Put all the ingredients in a large baking pan and stir to mix. Bake the vegetables in a moderate oven for approximately 1 1/2 hours. If necessary, add a little water during cooking.
Variation: You may also add feta cheese broken into little pieces.

# Papoutsakia Melitzanes
## Baked Stuffed Aubergines (Eggplant)

### SERVES 8

- 1 1/2 kg (3.3 lb) medium-sized aubergines (large purple type)
- 2 onions, finely chopped
- 1 cup olive oil
- 500 gr (17.6 oz) minced beef
- Salt, pepper
- 1/2 cup white unresinated wine
- Parsley, finely chopped
- Grated cheese
- Bechamel sauce (see Sauces)

Remove the stems from the aubergines, wash and cut them in half lengthwise. Incise the cut surface, rub the salt and let stand 1/2 hour. Rinse them off, pat them dry and put them, cut side down, in a baking pan with 1 cup hot water. Bake in a moderate oven for 15 minutes or until the aubergines are soft. Sauté the onions in a pot and add the minced meat, wine and parsley. Cook the mixture for 30 minutes over low heat. Remove the seeds and part of the flesh from the aubergines, fill them with the meat mixture and top with a spoonful of Bechamel sauce. Sprinkle with grated cheese. Bake for 30 - 40 minutes.
Note: Tomato juice may be poured into the pan with the aubergines to form a sauce.

# Gigantes Fournou
## Oven Roasted Giant Beans

### SERVES 6

- 500 gr (17.6 oz) dried giant white beans
- 3/4 cup olive oil
- 4 ripe tomatoes
- Parsley, finely chopped
- Salt, pepper

The evening before cooking, put the beans in water to soak. Next day, boil them until they are tender and drain them well. Peel and chop up the tomatoes, adding the salt, pepper, oil and parsley. Spread the beans out in a baking pan and pour the sauce over them. Bake for about 40 minutes. Serve hot or cold.
Note: The sauce may be boiled for a short time before adding it to the beans.

# Moussakas
## Moussakas

### SERVES 6 - 8
- 3 large aubergines (large purple type)
- 1 kg (2.2 lb) potatoes
- 1 onion, finely chopped
- 1 kg (2.2 lb) minced beef
- 1/2 cup white unresinated wine
- 1/2 cup olive oil
- 2 medium ripe tomatoes
- Parsley, finely chopped
- Salt, pepper
- Olive oil for frying
- Bechamel sauce (see Sauces)

Wrap the aubergines (eggplant) in aluminium foil and bake in a moderate oven until soft. Wash and peel the potatoes, slice them and fry them lightly. Heat the oil and sauté the onion with the minced beef. Add the wine and the tomatoes, which have been peeled and put through a food mill, the parsley, salt and pepper and let the meat sauce simmer for 15 minutes. Arrange the potatoes on the bottom of a baking pan, salt them and pour the meat sauce over them. Cover with the aubergines, sliced and salted. Top with a layer of Bechamel sauce. Bake the moussakas in a moderate oven for 30 - 40 minutes.

Note: According to the traditional recipe, the aubergines are fried instead of baked. This makes the dish heavier.

# Patatokeftedes
## Potato Patties

### SERVES 6
• 1 kg (2.2 lb) potatoes
• 300 gr (10.6 oz) grated kefalotiri cheese
• 2 eggs
• A little parsley, finely chopped
• Salt, pepper
• Olive oil for frying
• Flour

Wash and peel the potatoes. Boil them until they are soft and put them through a food mill. Place them in a bowl and add the cheese, eggs, parsley, pepper and a little salt. Knead the mixture well and shape it into patties. Dredge the patties in flour and fry them in hot oil until they are brown on both sides.
Variation: You can substitute feta cheese for the kefalotiri.

# Anginares alla Polita
## Artichokes in Olive Oil

### SERVES 4
• 8 artichokes
• 8 spring onions, finely chopped
• Juice of 2 lemons
• 500 gr (17.6 oz) small potatoes
• 4 carrots, sliced
• 1/2 cup olive oil
• 1 tablespoon flour
• 1 bunch dillweed, finely chopped
• Salt, pepper

Tear the tough leaves off the artichokes and remove the fuzz from their interior. Put them in a bowl of water, to which the juice of one lemon has been added, to keep them from turning black. Sauté the spring onions and the carrots, add the artichokes, dillweed, salt, pepper, the flour mixed with the rest of the lemon juice, and a good amount of water. When the artichokes are partly cooked, add the potatoes and continue cooking until all the vegetables are done.

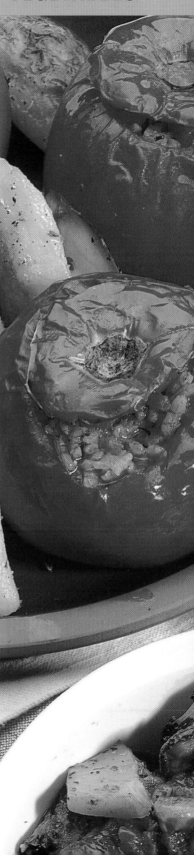

# Lahanodolmades Avgolemono
## Stuffed Cabbage Leaves with Egg and Lemon Sauce

### SERVES 6
- 1 large head of cabbage
- 500 gr (17.6 oz) minced beef
- 1/2 cup rice
- 1 onion, finely chopped
- Olive oil
- A little fresh dillweed
- Salt, pepper
- Egg and lemon sauce (see Sauces)

Remove the stem from the cabbage. Put it in a large pot of water and boil for 10 minutes. In a large bowl, mix the minced meat, rice, onion, dillweed, olive oil, salt and pepper and knead them well together. Separate the leaves of the cabbage and cut off any tough parts. Put a spoonful of the filling on each leaf, fold the sides over and roll up tightly. Line the bottom of the pot with a few cabbage leaves and arrange the cabbage rolls on top of them in circles. Place a rather heavy plate on top to keep them from opening as they boil. Cover the cabbage rolls with water and cook them over moderate heat for about one hour. Prepare the egg and lemon sauce, using the liquid from the pot. Serve hot with the egg and lemon sauce

# Kounoupidi Yahni
## Cauliflower in Tomato Sauce

### SERVES 4
- 1 1/2 kg (3.3 lb) cauliflower
- 3 onions, finely chopped
- 1 tin peeled tomatoes
- 2 cups olive oil
- Fresh dillweed, finely chopped
- Salt, pepper

Remove the leaves and main stem from the cauliflower and separate it into flowerets. Sauté the onions in the oil, add the tomatoes, salt, pepper and dillweed and bring to a boil. Add the cauliflower and cook for about 30 minutes. If necessary, add a little water during cooking. Serve hot or cold.

# Patates Fournou Ladorigani
## Oven-Roasted Potatoes with Olive Oil and Oregano

### SERVES 6
- 1 1/2 kg (3.3 lb) potatoes
- 1 cup olive oil
- Juice of 1 lemon
- Oregano
- Salt, pepper

Peel and wash the potatoes and cut them into thick slices. Put them in a baking pan with the oregano, salt and pepper and mix well. Pour in the oil, lemon and 3 cups of water. Cook the potatoes in a moderate oven for approximately one hour.

# Patates Yahni
## Potatoes in Tomato Sauce

### SERVES 6
- 1 1/2 kg (3.3 lb) small round potatoes
- 1 large onion, finely chopped
- 4 ripe tomatoes or 1 tin peeled tomatoes
- 1/2 cup olive oil
- 1 clove garlic, cut quarters
- Salt, pepper

Peel, wash and cut any larger potatoes into pieces the size of other smaller ones. In a pot, heat the oil and brown the onion. Add the tomatoes, peeled and put through a food mill, the garlic, salt, pepper and three cups water and let cook until the potatoes are tender and the sauce has thickened.

# Piperies me Saltsa
## Peppers in Sauce

### SERVES 5
- 1 kg (2.2 lb) sweet yellow peppers (long, tapering type)
- 4 ripe tomatoes, peeled and put through a food mill
- Salt, pepper, vinegar
- Olive oil for frying

Wash the peppers, pat them dry and prick them with a fork. Heat the oil and fry them until they are brown. Put the tomatoes, oil, salt and pepper in a pot and cook until all the liquid has evaporated. Arrange the peppers on a platter or ovenproof dish and sprinkle them with salt and a liberal amount of vinegar. Pour the sauce over them and serve hot or cold.

# Kounoupidi me Tiri sto Fourno
## Baked Cauliflower with Cheese

### SERVES 4
• 1 head cauliflower, approximately 2 kg (4.4 lb)
• 4 tablespoons vinegar
• 2 cups grated graviera (gruyere) cheese
• Salt, pepper
• Olive oil

Remove the leaves and main stem from the cauliflower and cut it in half. Wash the cauliflower thoroughly, place it in a pot with water, salt and the vinegar and boil for about 30 minutes. When it is tender remove it from the water and cut it into large pieces. Put it in a oiled glass baking dish, season with salt and pepper and pour the oil over it. Sprinkle the grated cheese over the top. Bake in a moderate oven until the cheese is golden brown. Serve hot.
Variation: You may use a variety of cheeses instead of just graviera.

# Anginares me Koukia
## Artichokes with Broad Beans

### SERVES 6
• 1 1/2 kg (3.3 lb) broad beans
• 6 artichokes
• 1/2 cup olive oil
• 6 spring onions, finely chopped
• 1 tin peeled tomatoes
• Fresh dillweed, finely chopped
• Salt, pepper

Wash and clean the broad beans. Remove the leaves and fuzz from the artichokes, cut them in half and rub them with lemon juice to keep them from turning black. Heat the oil in a pot and sauté the onions. Put the tomatoes through a food mill and place all the ingredients in the pot. Cover and cook for approximately one hour.

# Dolmadakia Avgolemono
## Stuffed Vine Leaves with Egg and Lemon Sauce

### SERVES 4 - 6

- 500 gr (17.6 oz) minced beef
- 250 gr (8.8 oz) grapevine leaves
- 1/2 cup rice
- 1 onion, finely chopped
- 1/2 cup olive oil
- Salt, pepper
- Egg and lemon sauce (see Sauces)

Remove the stems from the vine leaves. Boil them in salted water for 5 minutes. Let them drain for a few minutes. Put the meat, rice and onion in a bowl and knead them together to form a homogeneous mass. Put a spoonful of the filling on each leaf, fold over the sides and roll up. Arrange the stuffed vine leaves in concentric circles in a pot, add the oil and enough water to cover. Place a heavy plate on top to hold them down and prevent them from opening, and cook them for half an hour over moderate heat. Prepare the egg and lemon sauce, using the liquid the vine leaves were boiled in. Serve hot with egg and lemon sauce.

Note: If preserved vine leaves from a jar are used, they do not need to be blanched. They must, however, be washed well.

# Fava Santorinis

## Yellow Split Pea Purée, a Speciality of Santorini

### SERVES 8
• 500 gr (17.6 oz) yellow split peas
• 1 medium onion
• 1/2 cup olive oil
• Salt, pepper
• Parsley, finely chopped
• Onion, finely chopped
• Juice of 1 lemon

Wash the split peas, place them in a pot, cover with water and let them boil. Skim off the scum that forms on the top of the water. Add the onion, quartered, a little salt, half the olive oil, and let simmer for about an hour until the peas are soft and have acquired the consistency of thick porridge. Put the split peas through a food mill until they are a smooth puree. Add the rest of the oil, the lemon juice, the finely chopped onion and a little more salt. Stir and garnish with finely chopped parsley.

# Fassolakia Ladera me Patates

## Green Beans and Potatoes in Olive Oil

### SERVES 6
• 1 kg (2.2 lb) fresh green beans
• 1 large onion, grated
• 4 potatoes
• 4 ripe tomatoes or 1 tin peeled chopped tomatoes
• A little grated garlic
• Parsley, finely chopped
• Salt, pepper
• Pinch of sugar

Clean and wash the beans thoroughly. Heat the oil in a pot and sauté the onion. Add the remaining ingredients except the potatoes, along with a little water, and let simmer for 20 minutes, then add the potatoes, cut into quarters. If necessary, add a little more water and cook until well done. Serve lukewarm.
Variation: The sauteing of the onion may be omitted and all the ingredients placed in the pot at once. This makes the dish lighter.

# Manitaria me Saltsa Domatas
## Mushrooms in Tomato Sauce

### SERVES 4
• 500 gr (17.6 oz) mushrooms chopped into large pieces
• 2- 3 medium onions
• 250 gr (8.8 oz) white unresinated wine
• 1/2 cup olive oil
• A little rosemary and dillweed
• 1 bay leaf
• 2 cloves of garlic, finely chopped
• 1 tablespoon tomato paste
• Salt, pepper

Dissolve the tomato paste in a little water. Put it into a pot with the wine and olive oil and simmer for 10 minutes. Add the remaining ingredients and stir. Cook for about 20 minutes. Serve hot, after removing the bay leaf.

# Bamies Laderes
## Okra in Olive Oil

### SERVES 6
• 1 kg (2.2 lb) okra
• 1 cup olive oil
• 2 onions, finely chopped
• 4 ripe tomatoes
• Salt, pepper
• Vinegar

Trim the tops from the okra, wash well, sprinkle with vinegar and let stand for one hour. Rinse well and drain. Put the oil in a pot and sauté the onions and okra. Add the tomatoes, peeled and put through a food mill, the salt, pepper and a little water. Cook over medium heat until all the water has evaporated.
Note: Okra must not be stirred as it will break up.

# Fasolakia Xera Yahni
## Giant Beans in Tomato Sauce

### SERVES 6
• 500 gr (17.6 oz) dried white beans (giant size)
• 1 cup olive oil
• 3 onions, finely chopped
• 3 carrots, sliced
• 1/2 tin peeled and chopped tomatoes
• Parsley, finely chopped
• Salt, pepper

The evening before cooking, put the beans in water to soak. Next morning, boil them in plenty of water for about an hour, or until tender. Place the tomatoes, onions, carrots, salt, pepper, oil and parsley in a pot and simmer the sauce for half an hour. Put the beans in the pot with the sauce and cook for a few minutes.

# Domatokeftedes
## Tomato Patties, a Specialty of Santorini

### SERVES 4
• 500 gr (17.6 oz) ripe tomatoes
• 2 onions, finely chopped
• Mint and parsley, finely chopped
• Salt, pepper
• Flour
• Olive oil for frying

Peel and chop the tomatoes. Put them in a bowl along with the onions, mint, parsley salt and pepper, and mix well. Add flour until the mixture is soft but firm. Shape into patties. Put the oil in a frying pan, let it get very hot and put in the patties. Turn down the heat a little and let them brown in both sides, Serve hot. Variation: You may add grated cheese to the mixture.

# Melitzanes Laderes
## Aubergines (Eggplant) in Olive Oil

### SERVES 5

- 1 1/2 kg (3.3 lb) aubergines (long, narrow type)
- 4 ripe tomatoes, peeled and chopped fine
- 4 onions, finely chopped
- 1 bunch parsley, finely chopped
- 150 gr (5.3 oz) olive oil
- 1 whole bulb of garlic, finely chopped
- Salt, pepper
- Pinch of sugar

Clean the aubergines, cut them into pieces, rub them all over with plenty of salt and let them stand for about an hour. Put half the olive oil in a pot and sauté the onions. Add the tomatoes, parsley, garlic and pepper, and simmer. Rinse the aubergines in plenty of water and let them drain. Put the rest of the oil in a frying pan and when it is hot, fry the aubergines lightly.

Put the aubergines into the sauce and add water until they are half covered. Let them cook over low heat until the sauce is thick.

# Melitzanes Tiganites me Saltsa Domatas
## Fried Aubergines (Eggplant) with Tomato Sauce

### SERVES 5

- 1 1/2 kg (3.3 lb) aubergines (large purple type)
- 1/2 cup olive oil
- 6 ripe tomatoes
- 6 cloves garlic, finely chopped
- 1 teaspoon sugar
- A little flour
- A little white unresinated wine
- Salt, pepper
- Olive oil for frying

Cut the aubergines into round slices, rub them with plenty of salt and let them stand for approximately 1/2 hour. Rinse them off and set them aside to drain well. Dredge the aubergine slices in flour and fry until they are golden brown. Heat the 1/2 cup olive oil in a frying pan, sauté the garlic lightly and add the wine.

Add the tomatoes, peeled and put through a food mill, the sugar, salt and pepper and cook over medium heat until the sauce has thickened. Place the aubergines in a small metal or ovenproof glass dish and bake in a moderate oven for about 20 minutes, or until the aubergines have absorbed the sauce.

# fish

# Kalamarakia Gemista
## Stuffed Squid

### SERVES 6
- 1 kg (2.2 lb) medium-sized squid
- 1 cup rice
- 3 medium onions, finely chopped
- Mint, finely chopped
- Parsley, finely chopped
- Pinch of sugar
- 2- 3 tomatoes
- 1 cup olive oil
- Salt, pepper
- 2/3 cup white unresinated wine

Clean and wash the squid, and separate the tentacles from the bodies. Set the bodies aside and chop the tentacles fine. Heat a little olive oil and brown the onions. Add the parsley, mint, the squid tentacles, the tomatoes, peeled and put through a food mill, and the sugar and let the sauce simmer. Put in the rice, let boil for a few minutes and remove from the heat. Stuff the squid bodies with the mixture and sew them shut. Place them in a baking pan, pour the rest of the oil, the wine and a little water over them, and bake in a moderate oven for 25 minutes.

# Midia Gemista
## Stuffed Mussels, a Specialty of Constantinople

### SERVES 6
- 1 kg (2.2 lb) large mussels
- 1 cup olive oil
- 2 medium onions, finely chopped
- 1 cup rice
- 2 tablespoons pine nuts
- 2 tablespoons raisins
- Salt, pepper

Discard any mussels whose shells are open or broken. Rub those with closed shells with a stiff brush and cut their "beards". Wash them well under running water and drain them. Put them in a pot with a little water and steam until the shells open. Heat half the oil in a frying pan, steam until the shells open. Heat half the oil in a frying pan and sauté the onions lightly. Add the rice and sauté together for 1 - 2 minutes. Pour in a cup of the liquid in which the mussels were steamed (adding water if it is less than one cup), and add the salt, pepper, raisins and pine nuts. Boil the mixture for 5 minutes. Fill the mussels with the stuffing and put them into a pot with the rest of the oil and 1 1/2 cup of hot water. Cook over low heat until the rice is tender.
Variation: Add finely chopped parsley and mint to the filling.

# Barbounia me Saltsa Domatas
## Red Mullet in Tomato Sauce

### SERVES 5
- 1 kg (2.2 lb) red mullet
- Flour for frying
- Salt, pepper
- Juice of 1 lemon
- Olive oil for frying
- 1/2 cup olive oil
- 4 ripe tomatoes
- 1 clove garlic
- 1/2 cup white wine

Mix the flour, salt and pepper. Clean and wash the fish, sprinkle them with the lemon juice, dredge them in the flour and fry. Heat the oil and add the tomatoes, peeled and put through a food mill, the garlic and the wine, and simmer the sauce for 30 minutes. Place the fish in a baking pan, pour the sauce over them and bake in a moderate oven for 15 minutes.

# Astakos Scharas
## Grilled Lobster

### SERVES 4
- 2 lobsters, cut in half lengthwise
- Juice of 1 lemon
- Salt, pepper

Season the lobster halves with salt and pepper and place them on a hot grill, shell side down. Grill the lobsters for about 20 minutes, turn them over and grill for another 20 minutes. Serve with lemon juice or olive oil and lemon juice.

# Psari Fournou
## Baked Fish

### SERVES 4
• 1 kg (2.2 lb) fish (dentex, grouper, tunny, etc.), sliced into steaks
• 1/2 cup olive oil
• Salt, pepper
• Oregano

Wash the fish steaks, season with salt and pepper, rub them with oil and sprinkle oregano over them. Place them in an oiled baking pan and bake in a moderate oven for 35 - 40 minutes.

# Astakos Vrastos
## Boiled Lobster

### SERVES 4 - 6
• 1 large lobster
• 1 stalk of celery
• 1 carrot, sliced
• 1 onion, sliced
• 1 bay leaf
• 1 demitasse cup vinegar
• Salt
• Olive oil and lemon

Bring plenty of water to a boil in a large pot to which the vegetables, bay leaf, vinegar and salt have been added. As soon as it comes to a boil, put in the lobster, cover the pot and cook until done. Remove the meat from the lobster, cut it in slices and pour the oil and lemon over it.
Note: 1. If the lobster is still alive, tie its tail to its body.
2. A 1-kg (2.2 lb) lobster requires about 30 minutes to cook. Figure on 10 minutes for each additional kg (2.2 lb).
Variation: If the lobster has coral (eggs), you may add these to the oil and lemon dressing.

# Galeos Tiganitos me Skordalia
## Fried Tope with Garlic Sauce

### SERVES 5
• 1 kg (2.2 lb) tope, sliced into steaks
• Juice of 1 lemon
• Flour for frying
• Olive oil for frying
• Salt, pepper
• Garlic sauce (see Salads)

Mix the flour with the salt and pepper. Wash the fish steaks and sprinkle them with lemon juice. Dredge them in flour and fry them in plenty of hot oil. Dress with the garlic sauce and serve

# Marides Tiganites
## Fried Whitebait

### SERVES 4
• 500 gr (17.6 oz) whitebait
• 1 cup flour
• 2 lemons, quartered
• Olive oil for frying
• Salt

Wash the fish, dip them in flour and fry in plenty of hot oil. Season with the lemon quarters and serve hot.

# Marides me Saltsa Domatas
## Whitebait in Tomato Sauce

### SERVES 3 - 4
• 500 gr (17.6 oz) of the smallest whitebait
• 4 - 5 ripe tomatoes
• 2 cloves garlic, finely chopped
• Parsley, finely chopped
• 2 tablespoons vinegar
• 1/2 cup olive oil
• Salt, pepper
• Olive oil for frying

Wash the fish, flour them and fry them in plenty of hot oil. Peel the tomatoes and put them through a food mill. Place them in a pot, together with the garlic, parsley, vinegar, salt and pepper, and cook the sauce over low heat. Pour the sauce over the fish and serve.

# Kalamarakia Tiganita
## Fried Squid

### SERVES 4
• 1 kg (2.2 lb) small squid
• Flour
• Salt
• Olive oil for frying
• 2 lemons, halved

Mix the flour with the salt. Clean and wash the squid, dredge them in flour and fry in hot oil, turning them carefully so that they brown on all sides. Serve garnished with the lemon halves.

# Astakos me Saltsa Domatas
## Lobster in Tomato Sauce

### SERVES 4 - 6
• 1 large boiled lobster (see Boiled Lobster)
• 3 - 4 ripe tomatoes
• 1/2 cup olive oil
• 2 medium onions, sliced
• Parsley, finely chopped
• 1 1/2 cup of the liquid in which the lobster was boiled
• Salt, pepper

Remove the meat from the lobster and cut it in slices. Heat the oil in a pot and brown the onions. Add the tomatoes, peeled and put through a food mill, together with all the other ingredients, except the lobster, and simmer the sauce. When it has thickened, add the lobster, let it boil for a few moments and serve immediately.

# Karavides Ladolemono
## Crayfish with Oil and Lemon Dressing

### SERVES 4
• 1 kg (2.2 lb) crayfish
• Celery
• 1 medium onion, sliced
• Juice of one lemon
• Salt
• Olive Oil and lemon dressing (see Sauces)

Wash the crayfish. Place a little celery, the onion and lemon juice in a pot. Add water and salt and boil for 10 minutes. Add the crayfish and continue to cook over low heat for approximately 20 minutes. Drain the crayfish and serve with olive oil and lemon dressing.

# Gavros sto Fourno
## Baked Fresh Anchovies

### SERVES 4
• 1 kg (2.2 lb) fresh anchovies
• 1 teaspoon oregano
• 1 cup olive oil
• Juice of 2 lemons
• Salt, pepper

Clean the anchovies, cut off and discard their heads and wash them thoroughly. Arrange the anchovies in a baking pan with the rest of the ingredients and a little water, and bake in a moderate oven for 40 - 45 minutes.

# Midia Tiganita
## Fried Mussels

### SERVES 4
- 1 kg (2.2 lb) mussels
- 1 cup beer
- flour
- Olive oil for frying

Clean and wash the mussels as in the above recipe, "Stuffed Mussels". Remove the mussels from their shells. Dredge them in flour, dip each one in the beer and fry in plenty of hot oil. Serve hot.

# Psari Scharas
## Grilled Fish

### SERVES 4
- 1 kg (2.2 lb) large fish (pandoras, saddled bream, grouper, etc.)
- Olive Oil and lemon dressing
- Finely chopped parsley or oregano

Clean and wash the fish. Rub them with olive oil and lemon dressing and cook them under a hot grill. Serve with oil and lemon dressing to which finely chopped parsley or oregano has been added.

# Soupies me Spanaki
## Cuttlefish with Spinach

### SERVES 5
• 1 kg (2.2 lb) cuttlefish
• 1 cup olive oil
• 2 medium onions, sliced
• 1 clove garlic, finely chopped
• 3 - 4 ripe tomatoes or 1 tin peeled tomatoes
• Parsley, finely chopped
• Salt, pepper
• 1 kg (2.2 lb) spinach

Clean and wash the cuttlefish and cut them into small pieces. Heat the oil and sauté the onions and garlic. Add the cuttlefish, continue to sauté for a few minutes. Then add the tomatoes, peeled and put through a food mill, the salt and pepper, and simmer for 1 1/2 hour. Pick and wash the spinach, blanch it and chop it. Just before the cuttlefish are done, add the spinach and parsley and cook for a few minutes before serving.

# Garides me Kokini Saltsa kai Pilafi
## Shrimp with Tomato Sauce and Rice

### SERVES 5
• 1 kg (2.2 lb) shrimp
• Juice of half a lemon
• 1/2 cup olive oil
• 2 medium onions, finely chopped
• 1 clove garlic, finely chopped
• 3 - 4 tomatoes
• Pinch of sugar
• Salt, pepper, paprika
• 2 cups rice

Clean and wash the shrimp and simmer them for 5 minutes in water to which the lemon juice has been added. Drain them, reserving the liquid. Heat the oil and sauté the onion and garlic lightly. Add the tomatoes, peeled and put through a food mill, the parsley, sugar, salt, pepper and paprika and let the sauce simmer. Five minutes before removing from the heat, add the shrimp. Make up the liquid in which the shrimp were boiled to 3 1/2 cups with water. Add salt and put it on to boil. When it comes to a boil, add the rice, stir, cover the pot, reduce the heat to a minimum and let the rice simmer for 20 minutes. Pour the sauce over the rice and serve.

# Psari all Spetsiota
## Fish Baked in Tomato Sauce

### SERVES 5
- 1 1/2 kg (3.3 lb) fish (dentex, grouper, sea beam, etc.), sliced into steaks
- Juice of 1 lemon
- 6 ripe tomatoes
- 1 tablespoon tomato paste
- 3 cloves garlic, finely chopped
- Parsley, finely chopped
- 1 cup olive oil
- Salt, pepper
- Rusk crumbs

Wash the fish, sprinkle it with lemon juice, salt and pepper and place it in a baking pan. Peel half the tomatoes and put them through a food mill. Add the tomato paste dissolved in a little water, the garlic, parsley, olive oil, salt and pepper and stir. Pour the mixture over the fish. Slice the remaining tomatoes, place them on top of the fish, sprinkle with the rusk crumbs and bake in a moderate oven for about 40 minutes.

# Psari Vrasto
## Boiled Fish

### SERVES 4
- 1 kg (2.2 lb) fish suitable for boiling (dentex, sea beam, fresh cod, etc.)
- Juice of 1 lemon
- 2 carrots
- 1 medium onion
- Celery
- Parsley
- Red pepper
- Salt
- Oil and lemon dressing (see Sauces)
- To garnish: Boiled mixed vegetables (potatoes, carrots, courgettes, beets)

Clean and wash the fish. Place all the ingredients except the fish in a pot of water. Boil for another 20 minutes. Add the fish and continue to simmer for 20 minutes. Garnish with the boiled vegetables and serve with oil and lemon dressing.

# Bakaliaros Pastos Tiganitos
## Fried Salt Cod

### SERVES 4
- 500 gr (17.6 oz) salt cod
- 1 cup flour
- 1 egg, beaten
- Olive oil for frying
- Salt

The day before cooking, cut the cod into pieces and put it in plenty of water to soak. Change the water several times. Next day, remove the skin from the cod. Mix the flour with the salt, egg and water to make a thin batter. Dip each piece of fish in the batter and fry in hot oil.

# Bakaliaros Pastos Plaki
## Salt Cod in Tomato Sauce

### SERVES 4
- 1 salt cod
- 1 kg (2.2 lb) potatoes
- 1 cup olive oil
- 2 medium onions, finely chopped
- 4 ripe tomatoes
- 3 cloves garlic, finely chopped
- 1 bunch parsley, finely chopped
- Salt, pepper

The day before cooking, cut the cod in pieces and put it in plenty of water to soak. Change the water several times. Next day, drain the cod and remove the skin. Peel the potatoes and cut them into thin slices. Heat the oil and brown the onions. Add the tomatoes, peeled and put through a food mill, the garlic, parsley, salt and pepper. Arrange the potato slices in the bottom of a baking pan. Pour half the sauce over them, add the fish, and top with the rest of the sauce. Bake in a moderate oven for about 30 minutes.

# Kolii Psiti sto Fourno
## Oven-Baked Spanish Mackerel

### SERVES 4
- 1 kg Spanish mackerel
- 2 medium onions, finely chopped
- 3 ripe tomatoes
- 3 cloves garlic, finely chopped
- Salt, pepper
- Oregano
- 1 cup olive oil

Clean, wash and salt the fish. Peel the toma toes, chop them up fine and mix them with the rest of the ingredients, except the oil. Stuff the body cavities of the mackerel with the mixture. Arrange the fish in a baking pan, pour the olive oil over them and bake them in a moderate oven for approximately 40 minutes.

# Lithrini me Krassi
## Pandoras in Wine

### SERVES 6
- 1 1/2 kg (3.3 lb) pandoras
- 1/2 cup olive oil
- 3 small onions, sliced
- 3 - 4 ripe tomatoes
- 1 clove garlic, finely chopped
- Parsley, finely chopped
- 1 wineglass white unresinated wine
- Salt, pepper

Clean and wash the fish and place them in a baking pan. Heat the oil and sauté the onions. Add the tomatoes, peeled and put through a food mill, the garlic, parsley, salt, pepper and wine and cook the sauce for 30 minutes. Pour it over the fish and bake in a moderate oven for 30 minutes.

# Garides Ladolemono
## Shrimp with Oil and Lemon Dressing

### SERVES 4
- 1 kg (2.2 lb) shrimp
- 1 stalk celery
- Juice of half a lemon
- 1 small onion, sliced
- Salt
- Oil and lemon dressing with mustard (see Sauces)

Wash the shrimp. Put 4 cups of water in a pot with the celery, onion, lemon juice and salt, and boil for 10 minutes. Add the shrimp and simmer for another 10 minutes. Drain and clean the shrimp and pour the oil and lemon dressing over them.

# Htapodi me Makaronaki Kofto
## Octopus with Macaroni

### SERVES 6
- 1 1/2 kg (3.3 lb) octopus
- 1 cup olive oil
- 1 medium onion, finely chopped
- 1 clove garlic, finely chopped
- 1 wineglass white unresinated wine
- 3 - 4 ripe tomatoes or 1 tin peeled tomatoes
- 500 gr (17.6 oz) macaroni

Wash the octopus, place it in a pot (no water is necessary) and let it simmer until most of its juices have evaporated. Drain the octopus and cut it into small pieces. Heat the oil and sauté the onion, garlic and octopus pieces. Add the wine, the tomatoes, peeled and put through a food mill, the salt and pepper and cook over low heat. Add some more water and when it comes to a boil, add the macaroni. Serve when the macaroni is tender.

# Htapodi Vrasto
## Boiled Octopus

### SERVES 6 - 8
- 1 1/2 kg (3.3 lb) octopus
- 3 cloves of garlic, mashed to a paste
- Parsley, finely chopped
- Oregano
- Pepper
- 3/4 cup olive oil
- 1/2 cup vinegar

Wash the octopus and place it in a pot. Cook it over low heat until it is tender; no water needs to be added. Cut it into small pieces. Put the rest of the ingredients into a small glass jar, put the lid on and shake well. Pour the sauce over the octopus. It may be kept in a closed container in the refrigerator for several days.

# Htapodi Stifado
## Octopus Stew with Tiny Onions

### SERVES 6
- 1 1/2 kg (3.3 lb) octopus
- 1 cup olive oil
- 1 medium onion, finely chopped
- 1 clove garlic, finely chopped
- 1 wineglass white unresinated wine
- 3 - 4 ripe tomatoes or 1 tin peeled tomatoes
- 1 kg  (2.2 lb) tiny onions
- 3 tablespoons vinegar
- 1 bay leaf

Wash the octopus, place it in a pot and let it simmer until tender. It is not necessary to add water. Drain the octopus and cut it into small pieces. Heat the oil and sauté the onion, garlic and octopus. Add the wine, the tomatoes, peeled and put through a food mill, the onions, peeled and washed, the vinegar and the bay leaf. Let simmer until most of the liquid has evaporated.
Note: After peeling the onions, cut a small cross into the root end to keep them from splitting open as they boil.

# Htapodi Psito
## Baked Octopus, a Specialty of Thessaly

### SERVES 6
- 1 1/2 kg (3.3 lb) octopus
- 8 cloves garlic
- 8 bay leaves
- Parsley, finely chopped
- Olive Oil and vinegar

Wash the octopus. Place it on a large sheet of waxed paper and wrap up a clove of garlic and a bay leaf in each tentacle. Sprinkle the octopus with finely chopped parsley, wrap it in the waxed paper and place it in a baking pan. Pour a glass of water over it and bake it in a moderate oven for one hour. Serve with oil and vinegar dressing.

# Garides Tiganites
## Fried Shrimp

### SERVES 4
- 500 gr (17.6 oz) peeled shrimp
- 1 cup flour
- Salt, pepper
- Olive oil for frying
- 1 lemon, sliced

Mix the flour with the salt and pepper. Dredge the shrimp in flour and fry them in plenty of hot oil. Serve the shrimp garnished with slices of lemon.

poultry

# Kotopoulo me Hilopites
## Chicken and Noodles

### SERVES 4
- 1 medium-sized chicken
- 2 cups noodles
- 4 ripe tomatoes
- 2 onions, finely chopped
- 1/2 cup olive oil
- Pinch of oregano
- 1 green pepper, finely chopped
- 1 clove garlic, finely chopped
- Salt, pepper

Clean and wash the chicken and cut it into serving pieces. Put the tomatoes through a food mill. Heat the oil in a pot and sauté the chicken with the onions. Add the tomatoes, salt, pepper, oregano, green pepper and garlic and cook over low heat. Remove the chicken from the pot and keep it hot. Add 1 1/2 cup of water to the sauce and when it comes to a boil put in the noodles. When the noodles are almost done, put the chicken back into the pot, bring to a boil again and serve.

# Kotopoulo Psito
## Oven-Roasted Chicken

### SERVES 5 - 6
- 1 chicken about 1 1/2 kg (3.3 lb)
- 1 kg (2.2 lb) small round potatoes
- Juice of 2 lemons
- 1 cup olive oil
- 1 tablespoon mustard
- Thyme
- Salt, pepper

Wash the chicken thoroughly and rub it inside and out with salt, pepper and lemon juice. Rub the whole chicken with mustard. Peel and wash the potatoes. Place them in a roasting pan, season with salt, pepper and thyme and pour in the lemon juice, oil and a little water. Roast the chicken and potatoes in a moderate oven for 1 1/2 hour, turning the chicken over so that it browns on both sides.

# Trigonia me Pilafi
## Turtle Doves with Rice

### SERVES 4
• 4 turtle doves
• 1 cup olive oil
• 2 medium onions, finely chopped
• 1 wineglass white unresinated wine
• 6 ripe tomatoes
• 1 clove garlic, finely chopped
• 1 green pepper, finely chopped
• 2 cups rice
• Salt, pepper

Pluck, singe and wash the turtle doves. Heat the oil and brown the birds with the onions. Add the wine, the tomatoes, peeled and put through a food mill, the garlic, green pepper, salt, pepper and a few tablespoons of water, and let the doves simmer until they are tender. Place them on a platter with half their juice and keep them hot. Put the rest of the juice, the oil, 4 cups of water and a little salt into a small pot. Bring to a boil and add the rice. Reduce the heat, cover the pot and let simmer for 18 - 20 minutes. Put the rice on the platter with the birds and serve.

# Kotopoulo me Bamies
## Chicken with Okra

### SERVES 4 - 5
• 1 medium-sized chicken
•500 gr (17.6 oz) okra
•1 cup olive oil
• 4 - 5 ripe tomatoes or 1 tin peeled tomatoes
• 1 large onion, sliced
• Salt, pepper
• 2 - 3 tablespoons vinegar for the okra
• Parsley, finely chopped

Clean and wash the chicken and cut it into serving pieces. Heat the oil in a pot and brown the chicken pieces with the onions. Add the chopped tomatoes, salt and pepper and simmer. Trim the okra and wash it thoroughly, salt it, sprinkle the vinegar over it and let it stand for about 15 minutes. When the chicken is partially cooked, rinse the okra and add it to the chicken, together with the parsley. Cook until the sauce is thick.
Note: Do not stir the okra while cooking, as it tends to break up.

# Kotopoulo Lemonato
## Chicken with Lemon

### SERVES 4
- 1 medium-sized chicken
- 1/2 cup olive oil
- Salt, pepper
- Juice of 2 lemons

Wash the chicken and cut it into serving pieces. Heat the oil in a pot and sauté the chicken. Add the salt, pepper, lemon juice and 1 cup of water and cook over low heat for about an hour. Serve the chicken with French fried potatoes or rice.

# Kotopoulo Kokinisto
## Chicken in Tomato Sauce

### SERVES 4 - 5
- 1 chicken approximately 1 1/2 kg (3.3 lb)
- 1/2 cup olive oil
- 1 onion, finely chopped
- 1 tin chopped tomatoes
- Salt, pepper

Heat the oil in a pot and sauté the onion. Add the chicken, cut in serving pieces, and let it brown on all sides. Add the tomatoes, salt, pepper and 1/2 cup of water and simmer for about an hour. Serve with French fried potatoes or rice.
Variations:1. If desired, sliced green peppers may be added along with the tomatoes.
2. For a lighter meal, the skin and fat may be removed from the chicken before cooking.

# Agriopapia Gemisti
## Stuffed Wild Duck

### SERVES 4
- 1 wild duck
- 1/2 apple
- 1/2 cup olive oil

For the stuffing:
- 1 onion, finely chopped
- 300 gr (10.6 oz) sour apples, peeled and cut into cubes
- 1/2 tablespoon butter
- Celery, finely chopped
- 5 - 6 chestnuts, roasted and broken into pieces
- 1 small celeriac root

Pluck and singe the wild duck. Remove and discard the offal, reserving the liver. Wash the bird thoroughly and rub its body cavity with lemon, salt and pepper. Place the apple half and celeriac in the body cavity and sew it shut. Heat the oil in a pot, brown the duck , add a little water and let simmer until half cooked.  Take the duck out of the pot, remove the apple and celeriac from the body cavity and reserve the juice. Blanch the liver, chop it fine, add it to the stuffing ingredients and mix. Stuff the duck and sew the body cavity shut. Baste with butter and place in a roasting pan together with some of the reserved juice. Roast in a moderate oven for about an hour, basting from time to time with the pan juices.

# Ortikia Scharas
## Grilled Quail

### SERVES 4
- 1 large quail
- 1/2 cup olive oil
- 2 - 3 cloves garlic, sliced
- Salt, pepper

Pluck, singe and wash the quail. Cut through their breastbones, open them and pound them to flatten them up. Cut small slits in the quail meat and insert a slice of garlic, dredged in salt and pepper, in each slit. Season the quail with salt and pepper, brush them with oil and cook on the grill, turning from time to time.

# meat

# Arnaki Exohiko
## Lamb Country-Style

### SERVES 6
• 1 kg (2.2 lb) leg of lamb
• 2 onions, finely chopped
• 1 cup olive oil
• 200 gr (7 oz) kefalotiri or kefalograviera cheese, broken into small pieces
• Salt, pepper
• 6 sheets phyllo dough

Cut the meat into serving pieces and wash it. Cook the onion in a frying pan with a little water until it is soft. Add one teaspoon butter and sauté lightly. Add the meat, salt, and pepper and continue to sauté for a few more minutes. Remove the pan from the heat, add the cheese and divide the mixture into portions. Brush the dough with oil, one sheet at a time. Place one portion of the meat mixture on each sheet and fold it into a rectangular packet. Place the packets in a oiled baking pan, pour the remaining oil over them, and bake in a moderate oven for about an hour.

# Moshari Stifado
## Veal Stew with Tiny Onions

### SERVES 5 - 6
• 1 kg (2.2 lb) shoulder of veal (without bones)
• 1 medium onion, finely chopped
• 1 cup dry red wine
• 1 cup olive oil
• 4 ripe tomatoes
• 1tablespoon tomato paste
• 1 bay leaf
• Salt
• Whole peppercorns
• 1 kg (2.2 lb) tiny onions

Wash the meat and cut it into serving pieces. Heat the oil and sauté the meat. Add the onion and continue cooking. Next add the wine, the tomatoes, peeled and put through a food mill, the tomato paste mixed in a cup of water, the bay leaf, the salt, the pepper and about 1 1/2 cup of hot water. Cover the pot and let the meat simmer for 1 1/2 hours. Peel the onions and cut a small cross in their bases. Put the onions in the pot and continue cooking for another hour.

# Hirines Brizoles Krassates
## Pork Chops with Wine

### SERVES 4
- 4 pork chops
- 1 small glass white unresinated wine
- 1/2 cup olive oil
- Salt, pepper

Wash the chops. Heat the oil and fry the chops on both sides. Add the wine, salt and pepper, covering the frying pan and simmer over very low heat until most of the liquid has evaporated, and only the oil is left

# Arnaki Souvlas
## Spit-Roasted Lamb

- 1 lamb, 8-9 kg (17.6-19.8 lb)
- Olive oil
- 2 - 3 lemons
- Salt, pepper

Remove the lambs' entails including the larynx and large intestine, leaving the kidneys in place. Wash the lamb well and season the body cavity with salt and pepper. Skewer it carefully, from back to front. Fasten the backbone, neck and legs to the skewer with wire. Sew the belly shut. Rub the lamb all over with lemon juice, salt and pepper. Place it over the coals, which have been allowed to burn down. Turn the spit fast in the beginning and more slowly as the lamb cooks, until the skin is nice browned and it is done inside. As the lamb roasts, baste it with a mixture of oil and lemon juice.

113

# Arnaki Youvetsi
## Baked Lamb with Manestra

### SERVES 5
• 1 kg (2.2 lb) lamb
• 1/2 cup olive oil
• 1 onion, finely chopped
• 4 - 5 ripe tomatoes
• 500 gr (17.6 oz) manestra (rice-like pasta)
• Salt, pepper
• Pinch of sugar
• Grated cheese

Cut the lamb into pieces and sauté it in the oil. Add the onion and continue cooking. Peel the tomatoes, put them through a food mill and put them into the pot, along with the sugar, salt, and pepper. Cover the pot and let the lamb cook slowly for about an hour. Put the lamb and its sauce in an earthenware baking dish (youvetsi) or a baking pan, and add the manestra and hot water (3 cups of water for each cup of manestra). Stir well, sprinkle with grated cheese and bake in a moderate oven for 30 - 40 minutes.

# Arnaki me Anginares
## Lamb with Artichokes

### SERVES 5
• 1 kg (2.2 lb) shoulder or saddle of lamb
• 8 spring onions
• 1/2 cup olive oil
• 2 carrots, thinly sliced
• 5 artichokes
• 1 lemon
• Fresh dillweed, finely chopped
• Salt, pepper
• Egg and lemon sauce (see Sauces)

Wash the meat and cut it into serving pieces. Heat the butter, sauté the meat and season it with a sprinkling of salt and pepper. Add a little water and let the meat simmer for one hour. Put a little water into a pot, add the onion and let it cook until the water has evaporated. Remove the stems, leaves and fuzz from the artichokes, cut them in half and rub them with lemon juice. Add the artichokes, carrots, dillweed and onions to the meat and continue to cook for another 30 minutes. Prepare the egg and lemon sauce, pour it over the meat mixture and serve.

# Arnaki Atzem Pilafi
## Stewed Lamb with Rice

### SERVES 5
• 1 kg (2.2 lb) lamb shoulder
• 1/2 cup olive oil
• 1 onion, finely chopped
• 4 ripe tomatoes
• 2 cups rice
• Salt, pepper

Wash the lamb and cut it into serving pieces. Heat the oil and sauté the lamb pieces. Add the onion and continue cooking. Next add the tomatoes, which have been peeled and put through a food mill, the salt and the pepper. Cover the pot and let the lamb simmer for about one hour. Add 4 more cups of hot water and as soon as it comes to a boil add the rice and simmer for 18 - 20 minutes.

# Arnaki Gemisto
## Stuffed Lamb

• 1 small lamb, about 5 kg (11 lb)
• 1 set lamb offal (liver, heart, lungs, spleen, kidneys, sweetbreads)
• 1 bunch spring onions
• Fresh dillweed, finely chopped
• Fresh mint, finely chopped
• Feta cheese, not too salty, broken in pieces
• 3 cups rusk crumbs
• Olive oil
• Lemon
• Salt, pepper

Remove the head from the lamb. Wash the body, season it with salt and pepper, and rub it inside and out with lemon juice and olive oil. Bring the offal to a boil in a pot of water, drain it and cut it into small dice. Heat 2 tablespoons of olive oil and sauté the onions. Add the offal, the dillweed, the mint, salt and pepper and continue to sauté for a few minutes. Remove from the heat and stir in the cheese and rusk crumbs. Stuff the lamb and sew it shut. Put it in a roasting pan with a little water and roast it in a moderate oven for about 4 hours, basting it with its own juice from time to time.

# Arnaki Lemonato
## Lamb with Lemon

**SERVES 6 - 8**
- 1 1/2 kg (3.3 lb) leg of lamb
- olive oil
- Juice of 2 lemons
- 1 kg (2.2 lb) potatoes
- Olive oil for frying
- Salt, pepper

Wash the lamb, cut it into serving pieces and season it with salt and pepper. Heat the oil, brown the meat, add the lemon juice and a little water and let the lamb simmer for about 1 1/2 hour. Peel and slice the potatoes, salt them and fry them lightly. Just before the meat is done, add the potatoes, cover the pot and continue to cook until the lamb is tender and the potatoes are done.

# Arnaki me Kolokithakia
## Lamb with Courgettes (Zucchini Squash)

**SERVES 6 - 8**
- 1 1/2 kg (3.3 lb) lamb shoulder
- 4 - 5 tablespoons flour
- 4 - 5 tablespoons olive oil
- 1 onion, finely chopped
- 4 - 5 ripe tomatoes
- Parsley, finely chopped
- Salt, pepper
- 1 kg (2.2 lb) courgettes (zucchini squash)

Wash the meat and cut it into serving pieces. Mix the flour with the salt and pepper and dredge the lamb pieces in it. Heat half the oil and sauté the lamb pieces with the onion. Add the tomatoes, which have been peeled and put through a food mill, the parsley and some water. Cover the pot and let the lamb simmer for about an hour. Wash the courgettes and, unless they are tiny ones, cut them into small pieces. Heat the rest of the oil in a large frying pan and sauté the courgettes. Add them to the meat, cover the pot, shake it a few times and continue to cook for another 20-30 minutes.
Variation: Add salt and pepper to the courgettes as they are being sauté.

# Arnaki Fricassee me Maroulia
## Fricassee of Lamb with Lettuce

### SERVES 5
• 1 kg (2.2 lb) shoulder or saddle of lamb
• 1/2 kg (17.6 oz) spring onions, finely chopped
• 2 - 3 Romaine or Cos lettuces, thinly sliced
• 1/2 cup olive oil
• Egg and lemon sauce (see Sauces)

Cut the lamb into serving pieces. Heat the olive oil in a pot and sauté the meat. Add salt, pepper, the onions, lettuces, and a small amount of water. Cover the pot and let the fricassee simmer for about an hour. Prepare the egg and lemon sauce (with a little flour), pour it over the fricassee and serve.
Variations: 1. The onions can also be sautéed, but this makes the fricassee heavier.
2. Add finely chopped fresh dillweed.

# Sofrito
## Sofrito - a Specialty of Corfu

### SERVES 6
• 1 1/2 kg (3.3 lb) leg of veal (without bone)
• 4 - 4 tablespoons flour
• 1/2 cup olive oil
• 4- 5 tablespoons vinegar
• 3 cloves garlic, crushed
• Parsley, finely chopped
• Salt, pepper

Mix the flour with the salt and pepper. Cut the meat into slices and dredge it in the flour. Heat the oil in a frying pan and brown the meat. Transfer the meat to a pot, Put the vinegar, the garlic, the parsley and a little water into the frying pan. When this sauce has come to a boil, pour it over the meat. Cover the pot and simmer for 1 1/2 - 2 hours.

# Arnaki Kapama
## Lamb Ragout

### SERVES 6
- 1 1/2 kg (3.3 lb) leg or shoulder of lamb
- 1 onion, finely chopped
- Olive oil
- 4 - 5 ripe tomatoes
- Dash of cinnamon
- Pinch of sugar
- Salt, pepper

Wash the lamb and cut it into serving pieces. Heat the olive oil and brown the meat with the onion. Add the tomatoes, after peeling them, removing their seeds and putting them through a food mill. Add the cinnamon, sugar, salt, pepper and a little water, and cook slowly for about 1 1/2 hours.

# Gardoumbes
## Lamb Offal Wrapped in Intestines

### SERVES 4
- 1 set of lamb offal (liver, heart, lungs)
- Small intestines
- Sweetbreads
- 6 - 8 spring onions, finely chopped
- Fresh dillweed, finely chopped
- Parsley, finely chopped
- 3/4 cup olive oil
- Salt, pepper

Wash the intestines well, inside and out, and cut them into rather long strips. Cut the offal into pieces. Wrap up various pieces of the offal in the pieces of intestines. Put these into a roasting pan, add the onions, parsley and dillweed and sprinkle with salt and pepper. Pour the olive oil and a little water over the gardoumbes and roast them in a moderate oven, turning them from time to time until they are browned on all sides.

121

# Kefalaki Arniou sto Fourno
## Oven - Roasted Lambs' Head

### SERVES 2
- 2 lambs' heads split in half
- 1/2 cup olive oil
- Salt, pepper
- Lemon juice

Wash the heads, rub them with lemon juice and season them with salt and pepper. Put them in a roasting pan, cheek sides down. Pour the butter or margarine over them and roast them in a moderate oven, basting them from time to time with their own juices

# Splinadero
## Stuffed Large Intestine of Mutton

- 1 large intestine of lamb
- 1 set of mutton offal (excluding the lungs)
- Oregano
- 2-3 cloves garlic, finely chopped
- 50 gr (1.8 oz) kefalotiri cheese, cubed

Wash the intestine well, turning it inside out. Wash the offal, cut it into small pieces and sprinkle with oregano, salt and pepper. Mix the offal with the garlic and cheese cubes. Stuff the intestine with the mixture and roast it on a spit over charcoal or in a moderate oven for 1 1/2 hour.
Note : If itis roasted in the oven it showed be basted with a little olive oil.

# Bouti Arniou sto Harti
## Roast Leg of Lamb in Paper

### SERVES 6
- 1 leg of lamb, 1 1/2 kg (3.3 lb)
- 3 - 4 cloves garlic, sliced
- 2 tablespoons olive oil
- Salt, pepper
- 2 - 3 sheets of waxed paper

Wash the meat and cut slots in several places with the point of a knife. Insert a little butter and a sliver of garlic, dredged in salt and pepper into each slot. Season the joint with salt and pepper, rub it with olive and wrap it in the waxed paper. Tie it tightly with twine and roast it in a moderate oven for approximately two hours.

# Sikoti Arnissio Ladorigani
## Lamb Liver with Olive Oil and Oregano

### SERVES 4
- 1 kg (2.2 lb) lamb liver
- 1/2 cup olive oil
- Juice of one lemon
- Oregano
- Salt, pepper
- 1 bay leaf

Wash the liver, blanch, drain and cut it into small pieces. Place it in a pot, add the remaining ingredients together with a little water, and stir well. Let the liver simmer until it is done and and left only with the oil.

# Sikoti Mosharissio Tiganito
## Fried Veal Liver

### SERVES 5
• 1 kg (2.2 lb) veal liver
• Flour
• Olive oil for frying
• Salt, pepper
•  Lemon wedges

Wash the liver and slice it. Mix the salt and pepper with the flour. Dredge the liver in it and fry. Serve the liver garnished with lemon wedges.

# Arnaki Fournou
## Oven-Roasted Lamb

### SERVES 5
• 1 leg of lamb, 2 kg (4.4 lb)
• 2 - 3 cloves of garlic, sliced
• Olive oil
• Juice of 1 - 2 lemons
• Thyme
• Salt, pepper
• 1 kg (2.2 lb) potatoes)

Wash the meat. Make slits in several places with the point of a knife and insert slivers of garlic, seasoned with salt and pepper. Rub the joint with olive oil and place it in a roasting pan. Peel the potatoes, cut them into quarters and wash them. Sprinkle them with salt, pepper and thyme. Put them in the pan with the meat and pour the oil over them. Add the lemon juice. Roast the lamb with the potatoes in a moderate oven for two hours.

# Vodino Stifado
## Beef Stew with Tiny Onions

### SERVES 5 - 6
- 1 kg (2.2 lb) chuck or shin of beef
- 3 - 4 tablespoons flour
- 1/2 cup olive oil
- 1/2 cup red wine
- 2 cloves garlic
- Bay leaves
- 1 kg (2.2 lb) tiny onions
- 2 - 3 pieces of cinnamon bark
- 2 - 3 cloves
- 1 tablespoon tomato paste
- Salt, pepper

Cut the meat into large cubes. Mix the salt and pepper with the flour and dredge the meat in it. Heat the oil, sauté the meat and add the wine. Add the garlic, the bay leaves and three cups of hot water. Cover the pot and let the meat simmer until it is tender. Peel the onions and cut a small cross the root end of each one. Add the onions, the cinnamon and the cloves, along with the tomato paste mixed with 1/2 cup of hot water. Continue cooking for an hour longer.
Note: The onions may be satuéed in olive oil before they are added to the meat.

# Bekri Meze
## The Drinker's Appetizer

### SERVES 6 - 8
- 2 kg (4.4 lb) leg of veal (lean)
- 2 - 3 tablespoons olive oil
- 2 - 3 medium onions, finely chopped
- 2 - 3 cups dry red wine
- 2 cloves of garlic, crushed
- 1 bay leaf
- Whole peppercorns
- Cinnamon
- Allspice
- Oregano
- 1 tablespoon tomato paste
- 3 - 4 ripe tomatoes or 1 small tin tomatoes
- Parsley, finely chopped
- Salt, pepper

Wash the meat and cut it into large cubes. Heat the olive oil and brown the onion. Add the meat and spices and continue cooking. Add the wine, and then the tomato paste, the tomatoes and the parsley. Cover the pot and simmer for about 1 1/2 hour.
Note: If the sauce is too thin, add a little flour mixed with wine.

# Moshari me Araka
## Veal with Peas

### SERVES 6

- 1 kg (2.2 lb) of veal shoulder (without bones)
- 2 - 3 tablespoons flour
- 2 medium onions, finely chopped
- 2 medium carrots, grated
- 1/2 cup white unresinated wine
- 4 - 5 ripe tomatoes
- 2 - 3 sprigs of parsley
- Bay leaf
- 500 gr (17.6 oz) cooked peas
- Salt, pepper
- Olive oil

Mix the salt and pepper with the flour. Wash the meat, cut it into small pieces and dredge it in the flour. Heat the olive oil and brown the meat. Add the onions and carrots and continue to sauté.   Add the wine first, and then the tomatoes, peeled and put through a food mill, the parsley, the bay leaf, the salt and pepper and a good amount of water. Simmer the meat for about 1 1/2 hour. Add the peas and continue to cook for 10 more minutes.

# Moshari me Kolokithakia
## Veal with Courgettes (Zucchini Squash)

### SERVES 5 - 6

- Basic recipe Veal with Peas
- 1 kg (2.2 lb) small courgettes
- 2 tablespoons olive oil
- Salt, pepper

Prepare the veal as in Veal with Peas. Simmer the meat for 1 1/2 hour. Heat the olive oil in a large frying pan and sauté the courgettes. Add them to the meat in the pot and continue cooking for 20 - 30 minutes.

129

# Hirino me Fassolia
## Pork with White Beans

### SERVES 8 - 10
• 500 gr (17.6 oz) dried white beans
• 2 kg (4.4 lb) boneless pork
• 1/2 cup olive oil
• 2 medium onions, finely chopped
• 1 glass of tomato juice
• 1 - 2 stalks of celery
• Red pepper
• Salt, black pepper

The evening before cooking, put the beans in water to soak. Next morning, drain the beans and boil them until they are partially cooked. Wash the meat and cut it into serving pieces. Heat the oil and brown the meat with the onion. Add the tomato juice, celery, salt, black and red pepper, and let the meat cook for about 1 1/2 hour until it's tender. Add the beans and a little hot water and continue to boil for half an hour longer.

# Paidakia Arnissia Scharas
## Grilled Lamb Chops

### SERVES 4
• 1 1/2 kg (3.3 lb) lamb chops
• 1/2 cup olive oil
• Oregano
• Salt, pepper
• Lemon wedges

Wash the chops. Sprinkle oregano, salt and pepper over them. Brush them with olive oil and broil them under a hot grill.Serve garnished with lemon wedges.

# Katsiki Riganato
## Kid (Young Goat) in Oregano

### SERVES 6
- 1 1/2 kg (3.3 lb) kid (front end)
- 3- 4 cloves garlic, halved
- 1 cup olive oil
- Oregano
- Salt, pepper

Wash the meat and cut slots in several places with the point of a knife. Put half a clove of garlic, dredged in salt and pepper, into each slot. Season the meat with salt and pepper, place it in a roasting pan, pour the oil and a little water over it, sprinkle it with oregano and roast it in a slow to moderate oven for 2 - 2 1/2 hours.

# Katsiki Gemisto
## Stuffed Kid

### SERVES 6 - 8
- 1/2 kid (front end)
- 1 set offal
- 1 cup olive oil
- 500 gr (17.6 oz) spring onions, finely chopped
- Dillweed, finely chopped
- 1 - 2 ripe tomatoes

Blanch the offal, drain it and cut it into fine dice. Heat a little olive oil and sauté the offal, the onions and the dillweed. Add the tomatoes, peeled and chopped, the salt and pepper, and let the mixture cook until most of the liquid has evaporated.Wash the meat, season with salt and pepper, place the stuffing in the body cavity and sew it shut. Heat the rest of the olive oil in a large pot and brown the meat on all sides. Add a little water, cover the pot and cook over low heat until most of the liquid has evaporated and only the oil is left.

# Hirino me Selino
## Pork with Celeriac

### SERVES 5
- 1 kg (2.2 lb) pork shoulder
- Olive
- 2 tablespoons flour
- 1 cup white unresinated wine
- 1 kg (2.2 lb) celeriac
- Egg and lemon sauce (see Sauces)

Wash the meat and cut it into serving pieces. Heat the oil, brown the meat and sprinkle it with flour. Continue to sauté for a few minutes and then add 2 - 3 cups hot water and the wine. Cover the pot and let the meat simmer for an hour. Clean the celeriac and cut it into pieces. Blanch and drain the celeriac pieces and add them to the meat. Continue to cook for about 30 minutes. Prepare the egg and lemon sauce, pour it over the entrée and serve.

# Hirino Bouti Psito
## Roast Leg of Pork

### SERVES 8
- 2 kg (4,4 lb) leg of pork
- 1/2 cup olive oil
- Salt, pepper

Wash the meat, season it with salt and pepper and rub it with oil. Place it in a roasting pan, add a little water and cover with aluminium foil. Roast the joint in a moderate oven for 2 1/2 hours.

# Tas Kebab
## Lamb in Tomato Sauce

### SERVES 5 - 6
- 1 1/2 kg (3.3 lb) shoulder of lamb
- Olive oil
- 2 - 3 medium onions, finely chopped
- 1 small glass white wine
- 6 ripe tomatoes
- Salt, pepper

Remove the bones from the meat and cut it into small pieces. Heat the olive oil and sauté the meat. Add the onions and continue to sauté. Sprinkle with salt and pepper and add the wine. Peel the tomatoes, put them through a food mill and add them to the meat. Cover the pot and let the meat simmer for about an hour.

# Kelaidi
## Garlicked Veal with Green Peppers, A Specialty of Larissa

### SERVES 6 - 8
- 1 1/2 kg (3.3 lb) veal shoulder
- 500 gr (17.6 oz) green peppers
- 4 ripe tomatoes
- 1 whole bulb of garlic
- 250 gr (8.8 oz) feta cheese
- 250 gr (8.8 oz) olive oil
- Salt, pepper

Cut the meat, peppers, tomatoes and feta cheese into pieces. Put the meat in an earthenware baking dish, followed by a layer of peppers and a layer of tomato slices. Add the garlic, finely chopped, and the cheese, pour the melted olive oil over the dish, and sprinkle with salt and pepper. Bake in a slow oven until the meat is tender.

# Biftekia Scharas
## Grilled Meatballs

### SERVES 6
- 1 kg (2.2 lb) minced meat
- 1 cup rusk crumbs
- 1 egg
- 1 medium onion
- Parsley, finely chopped
- 1 tablespoon lemon juice
- Salt, pepper
- A little olive oil

Mix all the ingredients together, shape them into round patties about 1.5 cm (0.6 inches) thick, brush them with a little oil and cook them under the grill

# Souvlakia Hirino I Mosharissio
## Veal or Pork Shish Kebabs

### SERVES 5
- 1 kg (2.2 lb) lean veal or pork
- 1/2 cup olive oil
- Oregano
- Salt, pepper
- Paprika
- 3 green peppers
- 3 tomatoes
- 4 medium onions

Cut the meat into cubes. Place them in an earthenware or glass bowl and add the remaining ingredients, except the vegetables. Let the meat marinate for 3 - 4 hours. Cut the vegetables into uniform pieces. Skewer the meat, alternating with a different vegetable each time. Grill the kebabs over charcoal, basting them from time to time with the marinade.

# Brizoles Mosharissies Scharas
## Grilled Veal Chops

### SERVES 4
- 4 veal chops
- Olive oil
- Salt, pepper
- Lemon wedges

Wash the chops, brush them with oil, season with salt and pepper and cook them under a hot grill. Serve the chops garnished with lemon wedges.

# Moshari me Melitzanes
## Veal with Aubergines (Eggplant)

### SERVES 5 - 6
- 1 kg (2.2 lb) rump or leg of veal (without bone)
- 50 gr (1.8 oz) olive oil
- 2 medium onions, sliced
- 5 - 6 ripe tomatoes
- 1 clove garlic, finely chopped
- 1 1/2 kg (3.3 lb) aubergines (long, narrow type)
- Olive oil for frying
- Salt, pepper

Wash the meat and cut it into serving pieces. Heat the butter the sauté the meat with the onion. Add the tomatoes, peeled and put through a food mill, the garlic, the salt, pepper and a little water and let the meat simmer for about 2 hours. Cut the aubergines into thick slices and fry them in plenty of hot olive oil. Add them to the meat and continue to cook for a few minutes before serving.

# Soutzoukakia Smyrneika
## Smyrna Meat Rolls

### SERVES 4
- 500 gr (17.6 oz) minced meat
- 1 cup stale crustless bread
- Cumin
- Salt, pepper
- 4 ripe tomatoes
- 2 cloves garlic, crushed
- Pinch of sugar
- Olive oil for frying

Soak the bread and squeeze out all excess water. Mix the meat with the bread, garlic, cumin, salt and pepper. Knead the mixture and shape it into short sausage-shaped rolls. Fry them in the oil. Strain the oil and reserve about 1/2 cup. Put the meat rolls into a clean frying pan with the tomatoes, which have been peeled and put through a food mill. Add the sugar, season lightly with salt and pepper and let the sauce simmer for about 10 minutes. Add the meat rolls and cook a short while longer before serving

# Horiatika Loukanika Tiganita
## Fried Village Sausages

### SERVES 6
- 6 village-made sausages
- Olive oil for frying
- Lemon juice

Cut the sausages into thick slices. Fry them on all sides in hot oil, sprinkle them with lemon juice and serve.

139

# Keftedes Tiganiti
## Fried Meatballs

### SERVES 6 - 8
- 500 gr (17.6 oz) minced meat
- 500 gr (17.6 oz) minced pork
- 250 gr (8.8 oz) bread (crust removed)
- 2 eggs, beaten
- 2 medium onions, finely chopped
- Mint, finely chopped
- Oregano
- Salt, pepper
- Flour
- Olive oil for frying

Soak the bread and squeeze out all excess water. Mix the meat, bread, onion, eggs, mint, oregano, salt and pepper. Knead the mixture well and shape it into patties. Dredge them in flour and fry them in plenty of hot oil.

# Keftedes me Saltsa
## Meatballs in Tomato Sauce

### SERVES 6 - 8
- Fried Meatballs (see recipe above)
- 4 ripe tomatoes
- 1 tablespoon tomato paste
- 2 tablespoons olive oil
- 1 bay leaf
- Pinch of sugar
- Salt, pepper

Peel the tomatoes and put them through a food mill. Place them in a pot with a little water and all the other ingredients, except the meatballs, and simmer for 20 minutes. Add the meatballs, cook for a few minutes longer and serve.

## Splina Gemisti
### Stuffed Spleen

**SERVES 4**
- 1 large veal spleen
- 200 gr (7 oz) feta cheese, broken into pieces
- 1/2 cup rusk crumbs
- 3 cloves garlic, finely chopped
- Parsley, finely chopped
- 4 ripe tomatoes
- 1 cup olive oil
- Salt, pepper

Score the spleen and slit it lengthwise. Mix together the feta cheese, the rusk crumbs, garlic, parsley and a little olive oil. Season the mixture with salt and pepper, stuff the spleen and sew the opening shut. Place it in a roasting pan, and pour the olive oil and the tomatoes, which have been peeled and put through a food mill, over it. Cook the spleen in a moderate oven for about 50 minutes.

## Moshari me Bamies
### Veal with Okra

**SERVES 5 - 6**
- 1 kg (2.2 lb) shoulder of veal (bones removed)
- 1 kg (2.2 lb) okra
- 1 wineglass vinegar
- 3/4 cup olive oil
- 5 - 6 ripe tomatoes
- 1 onion, finely chopped
- Salt, pepper

Clean and wash the okra, mix it well with the vinegar and salt and let it stand for half an hour. Wash the meat and cut it into serving pieces. Heat the olive oil and brown the meat on all sides. Add the onion and continue to sauté. Add the tomatoes, which have been peeled and put through a food mill, together with the salt, pepper and a little water. Cover the pot and let the meat simmer for 1 to 1 1/2 hours. Rinse the okra well and put it in the pot with the meat, adding a little water if necessary. Cover the pot, give it a couple of shakes and simmer for 40 minutes.

# Moshari me Makaronaki Kofto
## Veal with Macaroni

### SERVES 6
• 1 kg (2.2 lb) veal shoulder (boneless)
• Olive oil
• 4 ripe tomatoes
• 500 gr (17.6 oz) macaroni
• Salt, pepper
• Pinch of sugar
• Grate cheese

Wash the meat, cut it into small pieces and sprinkle salt and pepper over it. Heat the olive oil and sauté the meat until it has browned on all sides. Add the tomatoes, peeled and put through a food mill, a little more salt and pepper, the sugar and a little water, and allow the meat to simmer for 1 1/2 hour.
Add as much water as is needed to boil the macaroni. When it comes to a boil, add the macaroni, stir, cover the pot, reduce the heat once more and continue simmering until the macaroni is cooked Serve with grated cheese.
Note: As the macaroni cooks, stir from time to time and add more hot water if necessary.

# Moshari Lemonato
## Veal with Lemon

### SERVES 5
• 1 kg (2.2 lb) round of veal
• Olive oil
• 1 bay leaf
• Juice of one lemon
• Salt, pepper
• Flour

Wash the meat and tie it. Heat the oil and brown the meat on all sides. Add a little water, the salt, pepper and bay leaf. Put the lid on the pot and let the meat simmer for about 2 hours. Mix a little flour in the lemon juice, add a little juice from the meat, mix well and pour over the meat. Let it cook a while longer and serve.

# Moshari Kokinisto
## Veal in Tomato Sauce

### SERVES 6
• 1 1/2 kg (3.3 lb) shoulder of veal
• 150 gr (5.3 oz)  and olive oil
• 1 small glass dry red wine
• 2 pieces of stick cinnamon
• 5 - 6 ripe tomatoes
• Salt, pepper

Wash the meat and cut it into serving  pieces. Heat the oil and brown the meat on all sides. Add the wine, followed by the tomatoes, peeled and put through a food mill, the salt, pepper, cinnamon and a little water. Cover the pot and let the meat simmer for about 2 hours, adding water when necessary.

# Miala Pane
## Breaded Brains

### SERVES 6
• 6 veal or beef brains
• Juice of 1 lemon
• 2 eggs beaten
• 250 gr (8.8 oz) rusk crumbs
• 250 gr (8.8 oz) olive oil
• Salt

Wash the brains and put them in a pot. Cover with salted water and let them stand for 20 minutes. Remove the outer membrane and place the brains in boiling water to which the lemon juice has been added. Let them simmer for 20 minutes, drain them and cut them into slices. Dip each slice first into the beaten egg and then into the rusk crumbs. Heat the olive oil and fry the brains.

143